Teaching in Your Tiara

a homeschooling book for the rest of us

Rebecca Frech

Printed and bound in the United States of America

To invite Rebecca Frech to speak at your event, visit **www.rebeccafrech.com**

Cover image: Joy Tolley
Cover design: Jon Benjamin

ISBN 978-06157915-0-0

Scabbed Knee Press ● Dallas

For my children-
who've taught me
everything I know
about learning

and

For my husband-
who's never read
this book

"There is no school equal to a decent home and no teacher equal to a virtuous parent."
— Mahatma Gandhi

"Parents give up their rights when they drop their children off at public school."
– Melinda Harmon, Federal Judge, 1996

Table of Contents

Foreward

Not too long ago, I prepared to start homeschool kindergarten with my oldest daughter (while I was pregnant with my fourth child – talk about taking on multiple life changing events simultaneously). What a time to be facing so many unknowns! I knew very few homeschoolers. I had no support structure. I didn't know what curricula were out there, let alone which was best. Most importantly, how in the world was I going to handle two toddlers and a newborn during school hours? Would she listen to me? Could she learn from me? Could I handle so many children and so much daily responsibility 24/7 without a break? Was I patient enough? Was I smart enough? Would I ruin my daughter for life? All of these burning questions, and I hadn't even gotten to the idea of teaching math. Math! I had struggled to learn it, so how would I be able to teach it to my daughter?

Then I met Rebecca. She listened to me, answered all my questions, brainstormed with me, calmed my fears, and was my sounding board.

At one point, Rebecca mentioned she was writing a book on homeschooling and asked me to read it. I jumped at the chance. She sent me each chapter as she completed it, and I eagerly devoured each one. Finally! Here was a mom who understood me! Better said, here is a mom just *like* me. She was passionate about her kids, committed to their education, and the development of rock-solid morals and values. Here was a mom who didn't have a completely organized and immaculate home, who hated messy crafts, who had been through the parenting and homeschooling gauntlet, and best of all - knew how it should turn out in the end: happy, well-adjusted kids who love their family, God and their neighbors – precisely what I so desperately want for my kids.

This book was exactly what I needed to read as a homeschooling tenderfoot. With her conversational writing style and calm, easy-going personality, it's less like reading a book and more like sitting down for coffee with a friend. She answered all my questions. Rebecca covers everything from different learning styles, avoiding (and coping with) common mistakes, how to maintain your own identity, how to deal with special learning issues, keeping up with the housework (I'm still working on that!), co-ops and groups, socialization, and so much more.

Thanks to Rebecca's book, I had access to her experience each and every day of my first year of homeschooling. We just recently finished our kindergarten year and I couldn't be happier – not only with the result, but with the entire process. My daughter has simply thrived in this environment, and I have the self-confidence to maintain that momentum for the years to come. I'm excited to continue our homeschool journey, including the addition of child number two, who is now on deck.

So kick your feet up, and prepare yourself for the start of an amazing journey as you read *Teaching in Your Tiara* – with Rebecca serving as your mentor, your guide, and your friend.

Beth Pack

Introduction

Twelve years ago, when I started thinking about teaching my children at home, I bought and read every book on the market about homeschooling. It didn't take long before I realized that those books were written for someone else.

Every book I read seemed to speak to some sort of paragon of woman-kind with an organized house, children whose clothes match, and a life that actually runs on a discernible schedule. I began to wonder if it was even possible for a regular mom like me to homeschool. I wasn't looking for someone to prove that I could be utterly successful. I just needed another less-than-flawless voice to say "I did it, and you can too."

It's been twelve years since my discouraging trip through the homeschooling section in the bookstore. I'm now the mom of seven, the eldest of whom is headed to college on scholarship. The youngest is still waddling around my house in diapers. I've got a dozen years of teaching under my belt – using six different curricula (two of which I designed) - I'm living proof that even the imperfect mother can teach her own children and do a not-half-bad-job of it.

You can do this even if:

- You've never thought about homeschooling before now

- You don't have 100 dreamy classroom ideas saved on Pinterest

- You aren't sure you could find a sharpened pencil in your house if your life depended on it

- You write notes to yourself in crayon

- You have no idea where you put those notes

- People ask if your children were potty-trained at 2 and you laugh so hard that you have to sit down

- It's a good week when the laundry gets folded, forget about the dream of it ending up neatly in the correct drawers

- The doctors in the Emergency Room know your children by name

- You've stopped those children from bleeding to death with bandages made from folded up tissue and packing tape.

- You keep buying Velcro sneakers for your kids because it's easier, and then realize that your 9 year old can't tie his shoes.

- Most days you'd much rather play dress up with the 5 year old and spin around the kitchen in a sparkly tiara than do just about anything else in the world.

If this sounds like you – and even if this merely scratches the surface – don't worry. There are more of us slightly wonky homeschooling moms in the world than you'd ever imagine. We're just as imperfect, spontaneous, fun, and just as successful as anyone else.

All I wanted twelve years ago was for a mom with a bit of homeschool experience to sit down with me at the kitchen table over a cup of hot tea and tell me the truth. I wanted answers to my questions. I wanted to hear about reality, not just a vague and picturesque ideal. I wanted to know both the good and the bad about how it really works and where to begin.

If you're looking for the same kind of real-world straight talk, then this is the book you need. Grab your cup o' tea, curl up on the couch, and let's get started.

ONE

Deciding to Do It

"I believe it would be much better for everyone if children were given their start in education at home." – Laura Ingalls Wilder

If you are anything like most parents who are pondering homeschooling, you're saying *"Am I crazy to think about homeschooling my children? What if I ruin them?"* That long list of all your fears about and arguments against teaching your children yourself is continuously running through your head. Those nagging doubts just won't go away and leave you in peace.

You're not alone with all those fears and arguments. Every homeschooling mom you'll ever meet has wrestled or is wrestling with those same fears. We all worry that we're going to mess up the kids. Then a moment comes when we realize that homeschooling is absolutely the best educational choice for our children, so we set the fear aside and do it anyway.

That fear of failure is a pretty good place to begin, so let's start there:

Will I ruin my children if I teach them at home?

In all my years of knowing and hanging out socially with homeschooling families, I have never met a "ruined" child. I have met many who have made life choices their parents wish they had not. I've met a few who ended up not being quite as well educated as their parents had planned they would be. I've met some very interesting and colorful characters, but not any who were "ruined." Ruined implies that you have reached the end of the road and there is nothing left to be done. If they're still breathing, there's still hope.

It's true that sometimes homeschooled children do not turn out to be the paragons their folks imagined they would be back in the beginning. While it does happen, it's far from the norm. But falling short of society's and most parents' definition of success seems to happen with a much smaller percentage of homeschooled children than among their traditionally schooled peers. The reason for this is very simple: – parents who accept responsibility for their children's education generally do just that; they make a commitment to their children and hold themselves to it.

The truth about parenting is that there are no guarantees about how your children will turn out in the end. Enrolling them in a traditional school, public or private, cannot and will not automatically guarantee success; neither does homeschooling.

Many variables will influence who your children become as grown-ups. Things like these:

- Their relationship with their parents

- Their relationships with their sibling(s)

- Their faith/moral upbringing

- How they view that faith/moral upbringing

- Their choice of friends

- Their peers

- The media

- The things they watch/read/enjoy

- Their dreams for themselves

- Your dreams for them

- How determined you are about those dreams for them

- Their relationship with extended family members

- Other adults in their lives

- Who they look up to and want to emulate (their heroes)

- Their education

- Their life experiences

The list of people and things that influence who your children become is seemingly endless. Of the many people and events that will direct and change the courses of their lives over time, education is only *one* of those things. It's an extremely important part, but it is only one part.

But how do I know if I'm the type of person who *should* do this?

There is not one type of parent who successfully homeschools and another type that fails at it. Homeschooling parents come in every type and variety. The biggest indicator of success I have seen has nothing to do with any sort of personality type. It has to do with liking your children. That's the first and most important question you ought to ask yourself: *Do you like being with your children?*

This question is one of the most difficult for parents, especially moms, to answer honestly. I know that you love your children. You might even say you adore them, or even that you're a bit mad about them. That's wonderful! Every child on Earth should have someone who loves them that way. That's not what I'm asking you.

I want to know if you enjoy spending a lot of time with them. Do you want to be around them? Do you miss them when they're gone? If they have plans with Grandma for the weekend, do you count down the time until they leave, or until they return to you? This is a vital point because *homeschooled children don't leave.* Your children are going to be in your house all day, every day. You will not be packing your small ones off on the school bus to send them anywhere. Are you okay with that?

Homeschooling moms (and dads) spend considerably more time with their children than they do with any other people – by a lot. If you decide to homeschool, you will be spending most of your day at home with your children (and in the car with them, and at the grocery store with them...you get the idea). *Are you okay with that?*

This is a foundational issue. The relationship you have with your children is the rock upon which you will build their education. Not enjoying spending time at home with the children is one of the most common reasons why parents quit homeschooling. They spend all of their time with their kids and they hate it. That doesn't mean that they are bad people or bad parents. It means they are human beings. We all have a point where we want to scream "TOO MUCH!!!" and you need to know where yours is.

If you're at all unsure about this, here's an easy experiment to try – Spend one whole week at home with your children. It doesn't really matter what you do with them while you're there –hang out, clean out the garage, blow up the baby pool, etc . The only catch is that during school hours there are no babysitters, no chatting on the phone with friends or texting, no drop-in visitors, no running around and doing. (For kindergarten and 1st grade, the general rule is 2-3 hours per day with an increase of half an hour per grade level.) Spend one week trying on the schedule of a homeschooling mom and see how it feels to you. Is it totally do-able or one of Dante's Circles of Hell? If you're leaning towards Hell, ask yourself why. What is it about being home all the time that's so bad? Is it something you can fix? For example, isolation can be lessened by giving yourself scheduled escapes, staying in contact with old friends, or finding a homeschooling mom with whom you can spend some time during the week in person or on the phone. I've yet to see an obstacle that a determined mother can't find a work-around for. If homeschooling is something you feel compelled to try, the way to do it is out there. You just might have to do some work to find it.

I'm with you on the liking them part, but I'm not sure I'm patient enough. What if there are days when I want to sell them all to the gypsies?

Are you patient enough right now? I don't know. The thing about patience is that it's like a muscle. The more you exercise it the stronger it gets. The only way to be a more patient person is to work at it. Are you going to fail sometimes? Probably.

There are no perfect parents in this world. There is no such thing as a mom who never loses it. We all do from time to time, but we work at it, and so should you. You're setting the example for your children of what adulthood should look like. You can look like an average mom, or you can strive to be holy. I aim for saintly every day because I want for them to be saintly. I don't want my children to be like me; I want them to be better.

Homeschooling parents aren't perfect people with infinite patience and halos hidden just out of view. There are days when we daydream about offices filled with grown-up conversation and wardrobes without cookie slime on the sleeves. We've all had days where we've hidden in the coat closet, called our best friend, and whispered, "I just need an adult voice. You have 5 minutes before they find me. Start talking!" Luckily for most of us, those days are the exceptions rather than the rule.

As for selling your kids to the gypsies, I've heard that they don't pay all that much for the little darlings. You'd be better off just raising your children until they're old enough to support you. I tell mine often how I'd like to be cared for in my golden years – I want to live at a spa and own a pony. They usually laugh, but I'm planting those seeds anyway.

What if I was never really a good student? Can I teach things I never really learned?

Many parents fret about this one. "What if I'm really bad at math? How can I teach my child at home?" I'll start by pointing out that you probably had a traditional education. (Unless you are the rare exception who was homeschooled; if so, then you should call your mom and discuss it with her.) If you are like me, you sat through years of math classes and came out on the other side not really understanding what you "learned" and unprepared for the higher level classes into which you were enrolled the following year.

Stop for a second and think about that. You went to a traditional school and didn't get it. You didn't get it to the point that it scares you to even think about teaching elementary math. You're worried about doing worse than the schools that educated you? – Is it possible to do worse than producing a student who is this scared about teaching 1+1? I don't see how.

You love your children and want them to succeed and will do anything to make that happen. Right? What if that means learning the math alongside them grade by grade? If you are not willing to do this, then you have your answer. You should not be homeschooling. See how easy that was to decide? If you gulped a big breath and said, "I can try...." Perfect! You're going to be better at this than you ever imagined.

The truth is that if you can read this book and follow basic directions, then you can teach your children. Remember that you will have the teacher's manuals if you need them. Teacher's manuals are like magic. They have all the answers, and many of them will even have scripts for you to follow. For years I've taught Latin, which I don't speak at all, because I can follow the script in the teacher's manual. If you look at your book and can't figure it out....Google is your friend.

I'm just worried he'll have all the same education issues I did. I struggled in history and was never great with Geometry.

We all have areas where we are stronger and places where we are weaker. Your son might have the same issues you do (especially if they are hereditary like dyslexia or learning disorders), but he also may not. He *will* have his own issues. There are no perfect people...remember? He will have his own unique academic weaknesses and some strengths you haven't even begun to imagine. History might be his favorite thing ever. Geometry might just make sense to him the first time through. You will not be able to predict what his every strength or weakness before you actually start teaching him. You just have to be willing to help him over any hurdles that arise along the way.

I just can't stop myself from thinking "12 years" – Can I really do this for 12 years? That just seems like an overwhelming commitment to make.

Committing to twelve years of homeschooling is an enormous step to take and I don't recommend that anyone do that. If you begin this journey with the firm and absolute resolution to homeschool exclusively until she leaves for college, *no matter what*...You are setting yourself up for burnout and panic. No one is asking you to make that kind of commitment and sign it in blood (if they are you should run really far away – that guy is creepy) or swear on a stack of anything. The only promise you have to make is for this one year, or even just this one semester. Maybe even just for this summer.

If at any time you think it isn't working, or that you or your children are miserable, nothing will stop you from putting them into some form of traditional school. You won't be betraying anyone by doing so. Homeschooling is not for every family, child, or parent. You have to make the decision about what's best for your situation.

Will he have opportunities that kids in school have – things like sports, clubs, prom, etc?

That depends entirely on where you live. If you live on a farm in the middle of the countryside, then I would think probably not. The upside is that he would be having experiences and opportunities that aren't available in town.

If you live in a medium-sized or larger city, then he probably will. Homeschooling has become so prevalent that most good-sized cities have groups, co-ops, and associations dedicated to re-creating the social aspects of traditional school for the homeschooling community. It will require a commitment and effort on your part to seek them out. You will be the person responsible for getting your child to and from practices and meetings. And these activities can be prohibitively expensive or a good distance away. Sometimes I feel like I'm living in my car. It's just a question of what's important to your family, and what you're willing to sacrifice to make it happen. You will have to decide that for yourself.

In some states, the public schools are required by law to allow homeschooled students to participate in all extracurricular activities, and sometimes even the classes you choose. (You people are so lucky!) It may still take some muscle on your part to make it happen for your children, but you have nothing to lose by making the effort. (You can find a list of the laws concerning homeschooling at www.hslda.org)

Can they get into college?

Yes! They absolutely can. Many colleges now actively pursue homeschooled students because of their higher graduation rates, lower remedial rates, and general preparedness. Don't take my word for it though, call your local university and ask the admissions department how they feel about homeschoolers. You'll find that they welcome you with open arms and great enthusiasm.

I'm a single working mom. – Can I homeschool my children?

Absolutely! I've known several single homeschooling moms. Their secret lies in arranging their lives in a way that makes educating their children at home possible for them. The moms of small children either work from home or teach them during their off hours. This can be very tiring, so make sure that you have the time and energy for it. Do a weeklong dry run. You are not doing them any favors if you are too exhausted to be nice or to actually do any work.

If your children are older, and you trust them to work independently, you can set up a syllabus for them to follow and then check their progress at the end of every day. Self-taught curricula and on-line learning make this much easier to do. Co-ops or study groups are also available for many students, so check your area to see what's near you.

Being a single homeschooling mom is not easy, but it is not impossible. You just have to set yourself up to succeed at it.

I'm still not sure if it's right for me and my family.

There's nothing I can say that will sway you one way or the other. I can only encourage you if this is what God is calling you to undertake. I suggest prayer and lots of it.

I'm a huge fan of asking God for guidance and requesting that He make it obvious. I don't know about you, but I've never been great with figuring out subtle. I need to be smacked upside the head sometimes. When my husband and I were pondering this decision, the more I asked God for clarity, the more obvious it became to us that this was where we were being led. God kept putting the right people in our path or the resources we needed fell into our hands. By the time that first school year came around, I was fairly certain that this was His plan for our family. I was still scared out of my wits, but I was willing to try because I knew He was leading me.

That's all He ever asks of us. He doesn't demand perfection. He just asks that we be willing to try.

That's the bottom line, and this is where it all begins. You have to like them and you have to be willing to give them the next year of your life. If you decide not to begin at all, that's okay too. This lifestyle choice, and it truly is a lifestyle, is definitely not for everyone. If it's not for you, I salute your honesty with yourself and wish you well on whatever you decide is best for your family.

Still interested? Good. Now you just have to make sure that Dad's on board with you. On to Chapter 2!

TWO

Talking to Dad

"I learned most, not from those who taught me but from those who talked with me." – St. Augustine

You've made it to Chapter 2! Which means you decided that not only do you like spending a huge amount of time with your children, but you are even willing to entertain the thought of spending all day every day with them—attempting to teach them at the same time. Good for you!

I think that I might really want to homeschool. What's my next step?

If you are very lucky, and much smarter than I am, you discussed and settled this issue long before you had children. (Bonus points if you discussed it before you were even engaged, you lucky duck!) If you and your spouse are already in agreement, hold his hand and squeeze it a little tighter. He's a keeper! Skip ahead to Chapter 3.

For the rest of us who didn't even think about this before the baby was born, or in my case before the day of the deadline to sign her up for preschool, it's okay. Don't panic. You're actually in the majority on this. Most homeschooling parents made the decision after one of their children was already attending a traditional school. Yes, the younger your children are the more time you will have, but you can still stop and consider all the alternatives even if the student in question will be in high school.

Start with a list. I find that sitting down and actually writing out my reasoning for doing something helps to clarify my thought process. I've lost count of the brilliant ideas which I gave up on once I looked at my thoughts on paper. It turned out that I wasn't quite as brilliant as I thought. Write it down. I find too that it helps to have a list of reasons neatly typed so that I can hand them to my husband. For some guy reason, he takes it more seriously in that format. So, type your list or write it neatly—this is one place where neatness counts. You may have to sell him on this, and a good looking presentation can't hurt.

The list I had for my husband all those years ago looked something like:

- She's only four and too small for all day preschool.
- She's already reading at a first grade level and the public schools won't teach to her level (There is no advanced placement in preschool where we lived.)
- I don't want her to be bored and the bad kid. That can follow her through her whole school career.
- She is crazy curious about the world around her. I've never met school kids who were that curious. I don't want that to die.

- She doesn't want to go. If you ask her, she'll say that she wants to stay home with the baby and me. I like being able to live on our own schedule. Our family works better that way. I'm not ready to be tied to a school calendar.

It wasn't the most brilliant list, but it was honest. I loved my girl and I wasn't ready to send her off for the day. Honestly, I never intended to be a "homeschooler". My not-even-thought-through plan was to teach her at home until maybe first grade. I simply wanted to enjoy just a little more time with her, so that's what I wrote.

Whatever your own reasoning is, put it on paper. While you're at it, ask Dad to make up a list of his own. Now that you've brought it up, what are his thoughts on homeschooling? Is he in favor of the idea, against it, or unsure what he thinks? Does he have reservations? What are they? Is it your ability or follow-through that has him questioning this decision, or is it his own lack of knowledge about the subject that's holding him back? Do the stereo-types and caricatures have him worried? Or is he concerned about putting more work on you?

Whatever his thoughts on the subject, hear him out. If his apprehension is rooted in his ignorance about homeschooling, point him to the same sources you found to be helpful. If you have done some serious research before broaching the subject with him, tell him that. Then give him some time to catch up to where you are in knowledge. Don't intimidate him by hitting him over the head with information before he has a chance to look into it himself.

But if he'd rather let you just explain it to him and answer his questions, then go for it!

If his problem is not so much with homeschooling itself but with the idea of you doing it, listen honestly to what he has to say. Few people know us as well as our spouses do. Is he worried that you have too much on your plate? Are you easily distracted or prone to bow to the whim of the moment? Is your life already overscheduled to the point where he doesn't see room for teaching? Do you have a difficult relationship with one or more of your children? Whatever his reservations, you should be willing to meet them head on and address them.

The goal of all of this is to get both of you onto the same side of the question. Take the time to discuss, and give him the gift of time and your patience while he thinks about it. Chances are that this bee has been in your bonnet for a while, but he may not have thought about it much at all. Give him time, and if all else fails, ask for a trial period.

How can you have a trial period with homeschooling?

It can be extremely difficult to make a decision about something you've never seen in person. Why not give homeschooling a shot for a set period of time and then decide what to do based on how it goes? I've made this suggestion many times to families who are considering teaching their children at home. Taking a period of time to test drive the homeschooling lifestyle will help you all be more comfortable with the idea – you, your husband, and the kids.

If your children are young, it's much easier. Preschool and sometimes kindergarten are not compulsory in most states. This gives you an easy semester or even an entire year to try it out before you have to commit to it on paper. If your child is of legal school age, you can easily use the summer or Christmas vacation if you'd like him to be able to return to a traditional school without losing time if this homeschooling experiment doesn't work. If you're up for a bigger challenge, try it for a semester. Nothing will prevent you from enrolling him in school at the end of the trial period if you feel that's a better option for your family. On the other hand, nothing will stop you from continuing to teach him at home if the trial period's a runaway success!

The rules for our trial period looked like this:

- I would research the grade level requirements for the grade our daughter would be in (This took approximately 15 minutes on the state board of education's website.)
- I would find a curriculum or textbooks that I thought would work for our child and our lifestyle.
- I would make lesson plans to cover the trial period (for us, it was preschool when our eldest was 4.)
- In the evenings, my husband would review our daughter's work with her so that he could see the progress she was making.

- At the end of every week, we would assess where we were in the books, how well it was going, anything either of us saw that wasn't working, and any adjustments we thought could make it better.
- Either one of us could at any time decide that the great experiment wasn't working and then we would move on to Plan B. (I had no Plan B. I just knew this was going to work. I'm pretty sure he had one.)

Your rules may look the same, or you may decide to throw mine away altogether and write your own. The point is that you need to have rules that you have agreed upon before you begin. This little bit of pre-planning will make the discussions along the way go so much more smoothly.

We don't live with my children's father. How much input does he get?

Unless your children's father is 100% not involved in their lives or you have made a reasoned decision that he gets no input in the education of his children, Dad needs to agree. A father who is antagonistic to your efforts will wear you out, put the children in the middle, and make homeschooling many times harder than you need for it to be. Divorce is not an automatic excuse for not discussing this with him. Your kids don't care about the dirty laundry, they do care about parents who are in agreement and present a united front on this issue at least. They deserve that, and you can do without the head ache. Talk to him and explain your reasons. He might just surprise you with how reasonable he can be.

What if we have the opposite situation? My husband wants me to homeschool our children and I'm not sure it's something I'm interested in doing.

This decision is one that can be determined by either two yeses or one no: you must both agree or the answer is no. It's that simple. If you are not in any way interested in teaching your children at home, then your family will not be blessed by your attempt. It will become a source of conflict and resentment within your household.

Before you just say no and walk away though, you should find out why this is so important to him, and actually listen to his reasons. Don't listen in the way where you listen just enough to be able to argue back. Actually listen to him. There is a reason why you chose to have children with this man, and I'd be willing to bet he's borderline brilliant. As he explains his reasons, if you can't stop yourself from adding in the "yeah, but..." then ask him to write it down for you. You won't regret giving him the courtesy of being sure to hear him out.

If his reasons are valid, and you're willing to consider it, then do a bit of research. This book is a good place to begin, but keep looking. Talk to women who homeschool and are willing to be honest about their experiences. Seek out women who have given it up and ask them why. Look at your life and make a fair assessment of how keeping your children home would change it. Are those changes ones you are willing to think of making? Would you be willing to give it a test run over the summer, or just for one semester?

If it's truly important to your husband, and you're not willing to teach, could you work? Are you capable of being the breadwinner for your family while Dad teaches the kids at home? If your earning potential or some other factor makes that a non-viable option, is there a way that you could supplement the education they receive in a traditional school?

The bottom line is that no one should be miserable in life. You have the right to not homeschool your children just as other parents have the right to do so. You shouldn't be pressured into anything, but hear him out before you start shaking your head no.

Supplementation could be a workable compromise. What would that look like?

Think of it as "homeschooling-lite". You would concentrate on a special interest or areas that need extra help and invest some time working on them. It doesn't need to be a big production, and for some areas it doesn't even need to be formal schooling. The goal is to give your children the extra help and attention they need to be able to thrive and do well in a traditional school setting.

For example, you might:

- Read classic literature such as *Black Beauty, Tom Sawyer,* or *The Chronicles of Narnia* either together or as bed-time stories and then discuss them. Think of it as your own family book club.
- Learn a foreign language together. Find a native speaker who is willing to teach your family, or learn from a curriculum such as Rosetta Stone.
- Teach your child's Sunday school class or even just help out in it. Continue the discussion throughout the rest of the week.
- Explore the local landmarks, memorials, and museums as a family. Find ones that relate to what he's learning in school and let him be your "tour guide."
- If your child is struggling with history, I highly recommend the Story of the World series. They read like a well written novel. Find the one that corresponds to the era your child is covering in school, then either read to/with him or have him read independently.
- For a child who is struggling with math in school, I really like Singapore Math as a supplement. The texts are easy to follow and understand, and are very reasonably priced. You can find them at any online bookseller. Simply match up the area she's struggling with to the corresponding lesson in Singapore for a little extra help.
- For an older, junior high or high school student, who needs math help, I'm in love with Teaching

Textbooks, a computer-based math program that does the lecturing, grades the work, and keeps track of progress for you. It's a little pricey, but much less than a private tutor.

- Attend cultural events like the ballet, opera, or art exhibitions and broaden your family's horizons.
  This doesn't have to be expensive. Most performing companies will have dress rehearsal or preview nights that are free to the public. You sign up on their websites for available tickets and then pick them up at Will Call on the date of the free performance.

There are endless possibilities out there for enriching your children's education. It just takes a bit of research and trial and error to find what works for your family. Don't be surprised if, while supplementing your children's education at home, you discover that you love teaching them and that homeschooling might be workable after all.

At the end of the day, your husband is not just the guy you married. He's also the father of these children you both love. Whether you're on the same page about homeschooling or not, you both want what is best for your children. Even when you don't see eye to eye, remember that you're at least looking in the same direction. You're a team. Try to keep that in mind as you move towards making this decision the only way you can – together.

THREE

Answering Questions from Dad

"Before I got married I had six theories about raising children; now, I have six children and no theories." – John Wilmot

My wife wants to homeschool our children, and I hear what she's saying, but I don't want to burden her with all that additional work and stress.

I love you. Is it okay to say that to you if I mean it in a completely platonic way? I love men who love their wives enough to worry about their workloads.

Homeschooling *is* a great deal of work *and* a gigantic responsibility. Nobody wants to see your wife work herself into a shadow of the woman you married. But, chances are, that if your wife is asking (pushing...begging...nagging...) to teach your children at home, it's because she thinks the sacrifice is worth it. If you agree with her, then the best thing you can do is to help ease her work load in other areas. Keep in mind that she will be taking on a full time job (teaching) in addition to the full time job (being a mom) she's already got. If she has *another* job outside of the house, she's really going to need your help.

Mothering a single school-age child is tiring. If there is more than one, it's exhausting. Add in the housework and errands, and it can drain a girl dry. School on top of that? It's a lot. But it's so worth it.

Will the house ever be clean again?

No. Not without your help it won't, at least not the way you've gotten used to seeing it. The level of mess and clutter a family creates when the children leave for the day versus the level of mess a family makes when the children are doing science in the kitchen and research projects in the living room are worlds apart. The greatest help you can give lies in not making her feel guilty about that. She knows the mess is there. She knows something needs to be done about it. This is a whole new way of living, which means a whole new way of organizing the house. That's a lot of new for her to take on all at once.

One of the hardest parts of reorganizing a house to fit in a learning space is figuring out where to begin. The other is getting lonely halfway through. Offer to help her figure it out on a weekend. Let her be the girl in charge – this is her office, and she'll know how she works best. Keep her company – that's so huge. As a general rule, women work happier when there's a great discussion to distract them from the work. Helping her out while talking with her for hours will win you amazing brownie points, plus it will help your house return to a new version of normal much, much faster. (See that? It's not the old version of normal, it's the *new* version. It's going to be different, but it can be pretty great.)

If she's teaching the kids, what is going to be required of me in terms of help, stress relief, or homework "check-ups?"

That's entirely up to your family. Let me tell you what works for us so that you have an example:

My husband is the Principal of our school. I can call him with discipline problems during the day, and he will speak with the offenders over the phone. There's nothing as scary to my children as the idea of "calling Dad." After dinner, he looks at what the kids have done during the day and discusses it with them. He helps with big projects, and drills math facts and spelling words. He's their audience for newly memorized poetry, and their cheerleader when they just aren't getting something. Above all, he trusts me to be the boss and lets me figure out how things work for each child. He's my sounding board and offers a distinctly different perspective. He has educated himself enough to know what's going on, but still lets me run the show without interference until and unless I ask for help.

Stress relief? That's where he *rocks*. He understands (because I've told him a million times) that I need to be able to clock out of work at the end of the day. What looks like a sweet time of snuggling the kids and reading bedtime stories is, for me, just one more book to read. I'm wiped out by the end of the day, so he does bedtime while I go and read a book to myself, watch TV, or take a bath. The decompression he does in the car on the way home isn't something I get to do until the children are in bed. I never get to be alone. Ever. The half hour of his tucking people in and saying prayers is his great and wonderful gift to me.

Please remember that what works for our family may not work for yours. Ask your wife what *she* needs. Don't just assume. (Trust me when I tell you that's annoying.) When she tells you what would help, try to do it if it's reasonable. Your wife is a smart lady (she married you after all), so believe her when she explains how you can make her life better, easier, and more-efficient.

How much input do I get or need to have? I can't remember Algebra to save my life.

Who can? It's hard to remember anything you haven't done in a while. The important thing is being willing to sit down and figure it out. If you're willing, not only can you learn anything, but you'll be an amazing example to your children. Learning is a life-long endeavor and worth the effort. What a blessing for them to have you show them that. For the things you can't remember – Google is your friend.

In the beginning especially, your wife *is* going to need your help. Sifting through the mountains of curriculum choices is daunting, and she could use the input of someone who knows the children as well as she does. You are an invaluable resource to her for catching the things she's missed and checking to ensure that all the courses are covered. You should have a passing familiarity with educational theory (get a book from the library) so as to be a reliable source of information. (A blank expression, shrugging shoulders, and "I don't know" are never helpful.)

How much and where you need to help will vary between families. Here are some places where you can offer to lend a hand:

- Be the Principal – Every school needs that figurehead for children to get sent to when they're not toeing the line. Can you be firm but fair, available for phone consultations, and conferences with the teacher to offer advice and a listening ear when things aren't running smoothly? You could be the principal of your very own school.

- Teacher – Every now and again, your wife is going to run into something that she's either worried about teaching or is a subject in which you are an expert. When this happens, how great would it be to have you as her go-to guy? Whether you are an engineer who can teach higher levels of math, a nurse who can help your children with dissection, or an amateur history buff who's dying to pass on your love for the Civil War, you have so much to offer your children. Your wife won't know that you're willing and even eager unless you tell her, so let her know!

- Tutor – There might be days (maybe longer) when no matter how hard your wife tries to explain something or how many approaches she tries, it's just not going to make sense to the child. Stop her before she throws her hands in the air and offer to give it a go. There's no relief quite like having help getting your children over the rough spots. Dads can't ever have enough chances to be the heroes to the women they love. This one may just be yours! Ask first, but then run with it!

- Field Trip Coordinator – There are amazing opportunities for learning available for your children – places you can go and things you can do as a family to help reinforce what they are learning in school. If you like doing those kinds of things, being the Field Trip guy could be your thing. Find out what your children will be learning in the coming weeks and find things in your area (or further out if you're up for a longer trip) that relate. Research it, check the schedule, and then make the plan! Go along to be the extra hands your wife wishes she had sometimes, and your wife will be the envy of the homeschool group. We've all wished, at least once, that we were married to this guy.

- Cheering Section – Everyone needs a cheerleader in her life. We need the person who cheers when we succeed and roots for us when we're the underdog. Your wife needs one too. Be this guy. Even if you're doing nothing else, be this guy.

There are thousands of other things you can do to assist your wife as she begins or continues homeschooling your children. Ask her what she needs, and then do what you can to help.

Not every dad is going to have the time and resources to help his wife as much as he or she would wish that he could. Some fathers have very demanding jobs that eat up huge amounts of time. You might have family obligations that require your attention and don't leave you with the time or energy to lend a hand. Still other dads are just not interested in being a part of the day-to-day of homeschooling. If a reason like one of these means that your wife will mainly be doing this on her own, be honest with her about that up front. Tell her what she can reasonably expect from you. If all you can be is the guy in her corner and the sympathetic ear at the end of a long day, please know that that kind of support is invaluable. While a hands-on dad makes homeschooling easier, not having one is not a deal killer. As long as you both have realistic expectations going in, you can make this work.

How much is this going to cost us?

(I tackle this in more detail in the curriculum chapter, but it's such a common concern of fathers, that I'm putting it here too.)

There is no exact number for what home education is going to cost. It can vary wildly from family to family depending on the curriculum choices you make, but the averages per student per year for a build-it-yourself curriculum are around:

Pre-K & Kindergarten – less than $100

Elementary School – $300

Middle School/Jr High – $400

High School – $500+

Boxed curriculum sets, where everything is provided for you, begin as inexpensively as $200 per year for Kindergarten (Catholic Heritage Curriculum) or as much as $500 or more for kindergarten (Seton). Generally speaking, the higher the grade level, the more expensive the curricula.

The more children you have, the less each successive year will cost you as they can re-use the books the bigger kids used.

Homeschooling isn't free, but it is much less expensive than private schools. It's even less than many public educations once you factor in supplies, wardrobe, transportation, and fees.

How do we make up for the income we'd lose by my wife's not working?

It depends on how much or how little she was making. You may not be losing as much as you think once you account for daycare costs, transportation to and from work, work clothes, and eating away from home. Before you panic and decide that you just can't afford this, sit down with a pencil and a calculator and figure out exactly how much income you will be losing, and what your budget needs really are. I'm not going to lie to you; you may have to cut back. Is homeschooling your children worth that kind of sacrifice to you? Is it worth it to your wife? Where do you draw the line? It sounds rhetorical, but it's a real question. If home education is important, and you are able to do it, you'll be willing to make sacrifices. If it's not a priority to you, you'll forever resent those cut-backs.

If there is no possible way to maintain your current standard of living on just your regular salary and you're not willing or able to change your expenditures, could one of you work part time? At one time my husband worked nights unloading shipping trucks from 10 p.m.-2 a.m. to make ends meet. It wasn't the most fun thing he's ever done, but it let me stay home during the day. Since then, my husband and I have both picked up side jobs and contract work from time to time to help cover expenses. I know of a homeschooling dad who spent his weekends doing odd jobs and painting houses. One mom in our homeschool group picks up weekend hours as a nurse, and another does freelance writing work to make ends meet. You'd be surprised how many creative wage earners there are in homeschool circles, and even more surprised at the crazy ways they have found to earn a little more money.

Sit down with your wife and the family budget and look for ways to cut back. It may be obvious things like forgoing that fancy coffee, getting rid of cable, or brown-bagging your lunch. Those things just jump right off the page. There are less obvious places, such as going vegetarian for a few meals a week because meat is expensive, having your wife cut your hair instead of going to the barbershop, or finding a church closer to home to save on gas. You'd be shocked at how quickly the little things can add up to serious money.

You may have to be creative either in your savings or your earnings in order to make this work. Don't be afraid to ask other homeschooling dads for ideas and advice. If they've been doing this for any length of time, they've become experts in how to make it feasible. Don't let it be a man thing. Ask. You won't be the first one, I'm sure of it. If home education is important for your family, then you *can* find a way.

Are we going to get in trouble for truancy? How do we prove that we're homeschoolers and not just parents letting their kids skip school?

With the ever-increasing numbers of homeschooled children around the country, this is rarely an issue unless you run into an over-zealous truant officer or an uneducated cop. The best thing you can do to avoid any problems is to know the laws in your state. You can find them at the Homeschool Legal Defense Fund website (www.hslda.org). If you haven't already become a member of HSLDA, it's definitely something to consider. For a yearly registration fee, you get free legal defense if you ever need it. If you live in a high-regulation state, it wouldn't be a bad idea to print off a wallet-sized copy of the laws and maybe even a copy of the form you used to register with your local school district (if you had to do so), laminate them, and keep them with you. You can also obtain a homeschool ID from many homeschool cover schools (like Seton or St Thomas Aquinas Academy) or from your local support group if you feel you need them.

If you or your wife are ever confronted, stand up for yourselves. Homeschooling is perfectly legal in all 50 states, so don't be afraid to say so. Follow HSLDA suggested guidelines and don't provide any more information than you are legally required to give. Get the officer's badge number and be sure to file a complaint if it's appropriate, but be courteous and respectful. Many people just don't know about homeschooling, and this is your opportunity to educate them.

If it truly worries you, you can cut down on the chances of being questioned by the local authorities by minimizing your visibility. This would mean not letting the children out to play in front of your house or at the park by themselves during school hours, not running errands with them until school is over, and just not taking them places traditionally schooled children don't frequent during the hours when you would be conspicuous. While I firmly believe that recess is important for growing bodies, they can run and play in the backyard, the basement, or even in the house (as long as no one wakes the baby). That said, we've *never had to use* these drastic measures. It turned out that the neighbors just didn't care what we were up to during school hours. I've talked to people all over the country and heard much the same. Unless you live next to a busy-body, you may be pleasantly surprised by how little other people are paying attention to what you're doing.

I played football (basketball, was in the band, etc.) when I was in high school and was looking forward to watching my son play too. Do I just have to give up on that?

No. You don't.

In some parts of the country, the public schools are compelled by law to allow homeschooled students to participate in extracurricular activities. If you are unsure of the laws where you live, check with your local support group or the HSLDA website. The local officials may not be aware of the regulations, especially if you're the first person to ask. It's worth it to check it out on your own.

If you're not fortunate enough to have access to the teams at your local school district, don't worry. Unless you live in a rural area, chances are that there are sporting activities for homeschooled kids somewhere near you. They may not be conveniently located, and you may have to make an effort to get your son there, but they exist. You may be called on to coach or to volunteer. Homeschool sports teams are generally parent-run organizations. You should be prepared to participate in some way, and possibly to buy his equipment. Being parent-led doesn't mean inferior teams, by the way. Our local team is coached by two former professional football players. I've seen the kids mop the field with the local prep school team. Several of the boys from last year's team went to college on sports scholarships. It can and does happen with stunning regularity.

If there isn't a homeschool sports league in your area, or it's not convenient for your family to be a member of the one that's there, there will be recreation and perhaps competitive sports teams that your kids can join. There are rec leagues for almost every sport you can imagine. This is a great option for kids to learn the rules of the game, experience being part of a team, meet other kids their age, and just play for the love of it. If your son or daughter is a talented athlete, rec teams can be a bridge to playing for a travel team or public or private high school if that's something you choose for them to do.

As an added bonus, homeschooled children are, on average, much healthier and more physically active than their traditionally schooled peers. They watch a LOT less TV, play fewer video games, spend more time outside, and just have more time to practice their favorite sports.

Having your children educated at home doesn't mean your daydreams for them have to die. The opportunities are out there; you might just have to be willing to work a little harder to make them happen.

What if I can see that it's not working?

If it's not working, or your wife's completely miserable, give her permission to quit. She'll beat up on herself a bit before she'll be willing to walk away completely. Be kind because she's going to be battle sore. She may need your permission to stop homeschooling, the actual words "It's okay for you to stop." It's possible that you might even need to suggest it to her. Do it gently. Let her know that deciding that homeschooling is not the best thing for your family isn't a failure on her part. It just means that you, as a family, need to change directions.

I just don't feel like a part of this at all. I leave for work and everything happens while I'm gone.

There are many times in homeschooling when it can begin to feel like "The Mom Show." Moms make the decisions, do the teaching, and run the whole thing. That can leave fathers wondering where they fit in within the greater scheme of their children's education. Rest assured, you have a place here. Your love, support, and as much help as you can offer are all essential in making sure that homeschooling is successful for your family. You are the rock your wife leans on and the approval your children crave. You absolutely have a place here, so be sure to step into your role.

FOUR

Talking to Family and Friends

"The way you help to heal the world is you start with your own family." – Bl. Mother Teresa of Calcutta

My husband and I are on the same page, but I'm worried about our parents. How do we break it to Grandma that we're not sending the kids to school?

I'm not a fan of "breaking it" to anyone. These are your children and you are responsible for their upbringing, no matter what your mother or mother-in-law has to say on the subject. I know that sounds harsh, especially if you're worried that she's going to rain down on your head for this, but there it is. Unless she's paying your bills, Grandma doesn't get a vote. Even then, I'm not sure I'd give her one.

Before you start wringing your hands and practicing your speech, consider the decent possibility that you are worrying needlessly. Your parents raised you and your husband to be the people you are. That means they know you better than most people do. This may not be as out of left field for them as you imagine it will be.

Even if they are surprised that you'd want to homeschool their grandchildren, that doesn't mean they will be automatically opposed to the idea. Your folks live in the same world you do, watch the same TV news, and maybe even read the same things you do. That means that you might be planning to say "We're homeschooling!" to people who are hoping like anything that you will.

If you're not one of the lucky ones with automatic family support, give them the benefit of the doubt anyway (unless experience teaches you otherwise.) It may not take as long as you think for them to warm up to the idea.

If you have a close and loving family, then whatever small hoops you have to jump through to keep your support network intact will be worth the effort. I've never met anyone with a supportive grandma who regretted the work it took to get her on board.

If your family is the not-so-supportive type, or has a history of questioning your parenting decisions, then you need a different approach. You may want to put off telling this kind of family for as long as possible. Less conflict might arise if you tell them once you're ready to begin than if you tell them in May, which gives them the whole summer to argue with you. Hopefully the fight will never come, but it doesn't hurt to be ready in case it does.

If your relationship with your family is complicated and prone to conflict, it is even more important that you and your husband are in agreement about this decision. There can't be one of you who is enthusiastic while the other is half-hearted. You need to be an impenetrable and united front in the face of manipulation, complaint, and general craziness.

If you have this kind of family, you know what it looks like and have probably figured out a strategy for dealing with them. Fall back on what works. If nothing works, then refuse to play the game with them. It's one of the benefits of being an adult which I love most: I can refuse to play the game. When someone is not so nice to you, change the subject or hang up the phone. This is your parade and no one can rain on it without your say-so... so don't say so.

My parents seem like they're on board, but then my dad starts in with the questions. This is beginning to feel like the Inquisition!

Slow your roll there, sister! Just because your dad is asking questions doesn't mean that he's not okay with the homeschooling. Most likely, he's just trying to understand something that's new to him. When your dad was the parent of school-age children, you sent them to school. The only choice was between public and private. The idea of just teaching them yourself is a bit revolutionary.

The good news is that you have parents who love your children. Do you know how blessed you are to have that in your life? They love them so much that they want to understand what you're doing with them. They just want to be reassured that their grand-babies are going to be all right. Please see this for the good thing that it is.

Most grandparent questions boil down to "Why?" and "How?" (Questions from strangers are pretty much the same, but they don't have any skin in the game. You don't owe them anything.) "Why are you doing this?" and "How is that going to work?" The grandfather, who needs a nap after taking your children to the park, can't imagine how you'll be able to get those little hellions to sit still for school. In his mind, it's a valid point. Be prepared for his questions so that you can easily reassure him. Even if he doesn't fully understand, he'll at least know that you've thought it through.

I highly recommend taking the time to think about those "Why?" and "How?" questions and write out the answers. Even if you are the only whoever sees that piece of paper, you need the reassurance that there actually *are* answers to those questions. You may want to re-write your answers every year. Things change. Your reasons for homeschooling *will* change. Make sure that you know what they are. A sense of purpose will keep you going on the days when you're ready to just walk away from it all.

Maybe the only reason you can think of is "God called me to this." But He called you for a specific reason. What was it? Do you have a special needs child who requires your focused attention at home? Does your family need the flexibility of homeschooling in order to have more time for other things? Are you just too scared to put your baby on the bus and watch someone else drive off with her? (Yup. This is a valid reason too. She's your baby. Wanting to be her mom is not wrong.)

Know your reasons. Research your methods. Be ready to answer well-intentioned questions kindly and patiently. And remember to be grateful that your children have grandparents who love them.

My mom is adamantly opposed to our decision to homeschool no matter what we say and is often hostile when the topic comes up in conversation (which is uncomfortably often right now). We used to have a great relationship. What's the deal?

For many years, my mother-in-law was deeply troubled by our decision to homeschool our children. Nothing we could say or do in those early years seemed to make a difference to her. She tried to reign herself in, but it was obvious that she had taken this choice of ours very personally. In those early years, I thought that I was the only one ever to encounter such fierce opposition from a grandma.

Twelve years later, I've learned that this is a common response from at least one set of parents, more often from the mom than the dad. In all the time I've spent watching one friend after another deal with this, I've come to realize that the most common cause of this reaction from grandparents is hurt feelings. (This is a great rule of thumb unless your parents are mentally unstable. If your folks are crazy, then all bets are off.)

Whether or not we intend it to be, a mother will too often hear the decision to homeschool as a criticism of her own parenting choices. She may just assume that you think she did a bad job with your education, which is why you've opted to take that left turn at Albuquerque. I don't know why mothers measure their own success by whether or not their kids emulate them when raising their own brood, but they do. If your mom is this kind of mom, this decision is going to sting a little – or a lot.

The best way to help her with this is with frank honesty. Do you think that you had a good education? If not, this is the time to tell her why (without pointing a finger of blame in her direction if at all possible!) Explain to her in real terms why you feel that this kind of education is in the best interests of your own children, and stress that they are your children if you need to do so. If your own school experience was great, tell her that too. Thank her for all of the hard work she poured into raising you and getting you to graduation. Then point out that it is because of the way that she raised you that you are capable of taking on this huge task and responsibility. Clearly, she didn't raise you to choose the easy way, but the right one. It also doesn't hurt to point out that if she were raising children in this modern age, she might just be making the same decision you are making.

Grandparents and extended family are a wonderful part of a child's upbringing. They are a support team that I sincerely wish every child had. You, the parent, are the coach of this support team. It's your job to help hold them together and to smooth the ruffled feathers. Getting all of this out on the table in the beginning will save you years of angst down the road. You owe it to yourself not to have to keep fighting this battle, so bury this hatchet now.

Having said all that, there is a point when you do get to cry "Enough!" and be done with it. If no amount of talking or patient understanding will even begin to get through, you absolutely have the right to stop discussing it. You're a grown up and the parent of your own children. As such, you get to decide when you are finished discussing and stick with that decision. It can be awkward and sometimes even painful to close the door and refuse to engage any longer, but sometimes you have to do it for your own sanity.

One of the hard and fast rules with our family has always been that no matter how much the grandparents question our choices, they don't get to do so in front of the children. Ever. I also do not allow anyone to play "Pop Quiz" with my kids to test their knowledge or to attempt to assess how good of a job I've been doing. At the end of the day, my husband and I are the parents and the decisions about how to educate our children are ours alone.

Please know that once they have a chance to see it all in action many loved ones come around. Homeschooling is just something they can't imagine until they see it. With honesty, understanding, and a bit of love it can happen. It took our parents seven years to get there. It can take what seems like forever, or it may happen overnight. I hope and pray that you get the right-away kind of support. If you don't, I pray that you have the patience and empathy to wait for it.

One last thought on family – In a perfect world, support for raising and educating your children would come from your family. That's the traditional picture we all have in our heads. For many of us, this just isn't the way the chips have fallen. While it can be a painful place to be, remember that all things, including support, come through Christ who strengthens us. Your support network will come through

Him and the friends He brings into your life. You will have the support you need – even if not in the way you expected – whether that support is found in your husband, your friends, online networks, or the lifelong friend you'll meet at the park tomorrow. Your people are out there, you just need to ask God to lead them to you (or you to them) and then trust in His perfect timing.

My friends and I all have children around the same ages. We used to hang out in playgroup and now we're homeroom moms together. I don't want homeschooling to change anything with my friends.

Things are going to change. If that's a big thing for you, then it's best that I tell you this right up front. Your relationships with the mothers of your children's friends will change. This is one of those truths in life: as our circumstances change, our friendships will change along with them. Do you remember when the first of your friends got married and suddenly hung out with other married people? The same thing probably happened when the first of your group had children, and didn't see as much of their non-parent friends. It happens, and it's okay. Sometimes difficult, but okay.

Unless you have something in common other than your children's ages, it's possible that homeschooling may end some of the relationships you have with the mothers of your children's schoolmates. Frankly, it was bound to happen eventually. Different teachers, moving to a new neighborhood, playing different sports...any of these changes may have brought about the end of the friendship eventually. It happens that way in life. There are friends we are meant to have forever, and those who only last for a season or two.

Unless you live in a very rural area, you will find homeschooling moms with whom you will have a lot in common. While they will not be a replacement for lifelong friends (at least not right away), they are your new peer group. Bonus for you! This is the perfect time for a little editing. The nice thing about gaining a new peer group while still having contact with an old one is that now you have options!

Take this opportunity to choose to surround yourself with people you genuinely like instead of simply the people who happen to be there. You have the luxury of looking at both groups and selecting which women you want to invest time in because you want to be friends with them, which you are content in just being friendly with at the occasional get-together, and which you'd rather not see at all. Figure out your own measure for friendship. I choose the people who make me laugh, bring the fun, and make me want to be a better me.

My best friend and I have been close forever. Now that I'm homeschooling she acts like I've shot her dog or something. What happened?

Just as parents feel judged by the choices we make for our children, our friends and acquaintances may feel the same sting. It is possible that in your saying "I've decided to homeschool." your mommy-peers will hear "I think I'm a better mom than you because I'm willing to do this and you aren't." Even if you've never even thought that, she may be hearing it.

This is the time to lay your cards on the table and ask her what's happened to your friendship. I hate confrontations like this, and I can feel the churning in my stomach just imagining it. I know it's hard, but it's completely worth the effort. She wouldn't have been your friend for so long if she wasn't worth it, right?

Suck it up, Buttercup, and just ask her. It may have nothing to do with your decision to homeschool, but if it does, it's better that you hear it now. Fix it if you can.

Okay, so I'm going to have a whole new group of people. I'm ready for them. Where are they?

Wouldn't it be great if there were a Tuesday night meet-up where all the homeschooling moms hung out and got to know each other? Then you could just look them over and pick the friends you want. If you're thinking "I wish," then I've gotta ask: why haven't you started one? (You're going to notice a theme about homeschooling – if you want it and can't find it, start it.)

If that's not your style, you might try these ideas:

- Check the online groups for park days, field trips, or other outings. Go to them!

- Take outings with your children and be willing to talk to any mom who looks like a likely friend. It sounds wacky, but I met one of my dearest friends in the grocery store check-out line. Talk to everyone!

- Once you've met the other moms once or twice, send out an email saying something like: "Moms' night out at the coffee shop – join us for coffee, friendship, support, and pie." I don't know what it is about pie that gets the moms to show up, but it's one of those rarely-fails marketing techniques.

- Look in your church bulletin for a homeschool contact number. Then call it!

- Send an email to the local homeschool groups and ask if there's anyone who'd like to hang out. People use the Internet for dating, why can't you use it to find friends? I've met some of the nicest people on Internet message boards for homeschoolers.

- No one said your friends all had to be homeschoolers. Look for people you have other things in common with. Is there someone in your Bible study class at church or your Latin dance class from the gym that you've always thought was interesting? Ask her if she'd like to hang out, and then go from there.

- Meet the people in your neighborhood. If you don't know everyone on your block, bake some cookies and go introduce yourself.

There are as many ways to find friends as there are people in the world. If you keep an open mind about it, and ask God for a bit of guidance, you will find the friendship and support you need. Sometimes that support is your own husband sitting there in your house. It might be the college roommate you lost touch with eons ago. Go find her! It might be the chick next door who looks nothing like you'd imagine your friends would look. I can't tell you where your friends are, just that you should go and find them. Good luck and enjoy the journey!

FIVE

Curricula

"The secret of teaching is to appear to have known all your life what you learned this afternoon. - Anonymous

Before we talk curricula, let's cover some terminology that every homeschooler should know. These terms define the teaching philosophies and types of curricula that the majority of homeschoolers use. Understanding the language of homeschooling will help you as you decide which curricula will suit you and your children best. Figuring out *how* you want to teach can help you figure out *what* to teach.

These are the most common basic teaching philosophies:

School at Home

School at Home is exactly what it sounds like; it mimics what goes on in the classroom of a traditional school. Subjects are taught separately, and the content is determined solely by the teacher. Mom is driving this bus for sure!

School at home has set class times, lesson plans, and schedules. Lecturing is done from textbooks, and the students have quizzes, reviews, tests, and sometimes even homework. This is what most people who are not familiar with educating children at home picture in their heads as homeschooling. It's children at desks from 8–3 diligently working while mom lectures and oversees their progress.

Montessori

The Montessori Method of education is usually associated with the teaching of very young children. It's based on the work of Dr Maria Montessori, who proposed that learning happens when children have freedom to discover within a structured and safe environment. The Montessori Method focuses not just on academics, but also on the physical and psychological facets of children. Taking advantage of their natural curiosity, this method calls for a classroom full of sensory materials (different textures, different sounds, etc.) through which students explore and learn. This is sometimes referred to as natural or unconscious learning. If this is something that interests you, go right to the source and read Dr Montessori's books on education. Even if you don't exclusively teach with the Montessori Method, her ideas can be easily folded into other educational styles.

Charlotte Mason

The Charlotte Mason Method of teaching has become wildly popular among homeschooling parents. Miss Mason's philosophy strongly emphasizes the idea that children are unique persons who should be respected and treated as such. This method uses what are known as "living books," books written by a single author with a passion for the subject, as opposed to dry textbooks, so that the subjects studied come alive. Miss Mason believed that children should be given thoughts and ideas in addition to facts. She also thought children should be encouraged to spend time outside discovering the world, and that an education should teach the whole child and not just his mind. If you are interested in learning more about her methods and philosophies, you can find her books online and in most libraries.

Classical Education

A Classical Education is a traditional method of training the brain to think and the child to communicate. It uses a three-part approach, called The Trivium, that leverages the three developmental stages children go through as they mature. The early years of school, called the grammar stage, when children's brains are sponges for memorization, are focused on becoming familiar with places and names and in memorizing facts and learning poetry. Around fifth grade, students move on to the logic stage where they begin learning how to piece the things they know together using logic and reason. Students at this stage learn to analyze information and draw conclusions from it. In high school, or the rhetoric stage, students learn to write with logic, force, and originality. A Classical Education is word-based rather than visually based – teaching is done through literature, discussion, and writing rather than pictures and images. If this appeals to you, the go-to reads on this topic are Susan Wise Bauer's *The Well*

Trained Mind and Dorothy Sayers's *The Lost Tools of Learning*.

Accelerated

There are many parents who look at the extra time left over at the end of the teaching day, and decide that there's no reason not to just keep going. Their children will often accomplish several years' worth of work in a single academic year. The students in an accelerated educational plan often graduate very early and go on to college, either traditional or homeschool, or begin working.

Delayed Academics

Just like it sounds, this philosophy is the opposite of the accelerated way of teaching. Parents who decide to use delayed academics feel that there is plenty of time to get to traditional schoolwork, and that the work of young children is to explore and learn from the world around them. This is a very gentle approach to teaching and can work well. If you are interested in learning more about it, take a look at the book *Better Late Than Early* by Raymond Moore.

Eclectic

After a few years of teaching their children, most homeschoolers settle into a more eclectic style. They may, for example, use Charlotte Mason for teaching history and literature, but a more traditional school approach for math and science. You will find that some of these approaches are easily used in tandem. Like most other parts of homeschooling, the more comfortable you become with what you're doing, the more you will tailor it to meet your family's learning needs and the way you teach best. No one can tell you what that will look like. You will discover it as you go.

We can't leave this section on teaching philosophies without mentioning **Unschooling**. Unschooling is not associated with a particular type of curriculum, rather it is a style of teaching that enjoys a wide popularity in the homeschooling community. Also referred to as child-led, interest-driven, or self-directed learning, Unschooling follows the natural curiosities of children and lets the student pursue those interests wherever they lead. It is similar in structure to thematic studies with the main difference being that the areas of study are decided upon by the student instead of the teacher. Unschooling works extremely well for motivated and interested students. Regardless of how the name sounds, Unschooling is not neglecting to teach. It often requires more time and effort on the part of the parents than any other teaching choice. It is museums, extensive research in the library, hours of reading and helping with the latest interests, and seeking out experts who are willing to teach or share their knowledge. It is *not* hanging out and playing Halo in pajamas all day or watching reality TV all afternoon.

Now let's try to make sense of all the curricula available for homeschoolers. (Have you seen the Rainbow Resource curriculum catalog? The New York City phone book has nothing on it.) I've identified six basic kinds of curricula as follows:

Traditional Curriculum – A traditional curriculum is the basic textbook and workbook kind of education you probably remember from when you were in school. There are 5-8 subjects for each grade, and different books for each subject. This is what is most common and appears in most boxed and packaged curriculum sets. It really *is* School at Home.

Due to the number of books required, a Traditional Curriculum can get to be pretty expensive. It's also time consuming and can be a little overwhelming because of the amount of book work involved. You might want to take a closer look at Traditional Curricula if any of these apply to you:

- You're a mom who thrives on structure and predictability

- Your student likes/needs structure and predictability

- Your child has been in school before and did well with the routine

- You're nervous about leaving something out

- You think your child may be back in a brick-and-mortar school in another year

Affiliated Curriculum or Distance Learning Academy – Some Traditional Curricula are offered by Distance Learning Academies such as Seton, Kolbe, and k12. These are private accredited schools with certified teachers and a set course of study. Distance Learning Academies provide several benefits to your family homeschool:

- Professional teaching staff and help when you need it

- At some schools, advice for tailoring the curriculum to your family

- Record keeping and official transcripts

- Assessment testing

- Special education guidance

Being an affiliate of a distance learning academy offers you a safety-net to make sure you don't miss anything. And, if you're a slacker mom, they can give you the accountability you need.

Thematic or Unit Studies – Thematic or unit studies, also called integrated learning, introduce multiple school subjects to the student through one topic, historical period, or subject. An example of this would be using the story of Peter Rabbit to teach about history (researching Victorian England, the time when the story takes place), math (how many bunnies there are), science (what's growing in Mr. McGregor's garden), nutrition (having a lunch of all the things Peter and his family ate) and language arts (the rhyming words such as Flopsy and Mopsy). Theme studies are great for the super creative moms and for those trying to combine grades. They also require a lot of flexibility on the part of both mom and student as well as a sense of fun and adventure. If you're creativity-challenged like me, Hands of a Child (handsofachild.com) will make you feel like a creative genius!

Keep in mind that with a Unit Studies approach to schooling, you will probably need separate math and reading/phonics books. This is a great choice for moms and/or children who have a hard time sitting still or prefer hands-on learning. Unit studies also make great add-ons to a Traditional Curriculum.

Programmed Studies – Programmed Studies are self-paced and sequential workbooks. The student starts at the beginning of the book and does a set amount every day until the end. The books can be designed to be used this way or can be the curriculum from a traditional curriculum used in this manner. Programmed studies take very little planning or preparation from mom and only require that the child be able to read, write, and follow directions. This works well for:

- A student who thrives on routines and loves workbooks

- A student who is able to sit still and remain focused with little supervision

- A mom who has just had a baby or is dealing with other issues

- A mom who has distractions which keep her from being able to continuously monitor the progress of older children

Classical Curriculum – I mentioned it above in teaching styles, and here it is again! It's both a teaching style and a curriculum category.

The classical curriculum relies on "The Trivium", a three-pronged approach to learning that uses the natural progression of children's cognitive development. These are:

- Grammar Stage (elementary school) – Harnesses small children's natural ability to absorb, memorize, and recall information. During the grammar years, children are exposed to songs, stories, and recitations that help them to discover the world around them. They learn the rules – phonics, math facts, Bible stories, prayers, spelling, history, classic literature, and Latin. (Yes, Latin.)

- Logic Stage (middle school) – Pre-teens are naturally inclined to question and argue, and the Logic Stage makes good use of that energy. Using the Socratic method, the formal study of logic, and debate; students are taught to look for and recognize the truth, think scientifically, and figure out how facts work together. They continue their study of Latin and begin learning Greek

- Rhetoric Stage (high school) – The Rhetoric Stage combines the knowledge and reasoning skills of the first two stages and brings them together. Students are encouraged to begin applying what they have learned to their own lives. They begin to specialize in branches of knowledge that interest them.

This is a good choice for moms and students who like books and logic with the added bonus of the creativity of unit studies. All the information a child learns is word-based through either the written or spoken word. This is wonderful for a visual or auditory learner, but can be very frustrating for a kid who needs to be more hands-on to learn.

Technology Learning – Technology learning is any program that is internet or software-based. It can be used as either an entire year's course of study or for a single class. This works well for:

- Students with learning disorders

- Students who do well with technology

- The mom who doesn't feel confident in her teaching *at all*

- Students who need to be independent for some reason (like being a teenager)

Another benefit, if you choose the online classes, is having the social interactions of "virtual classmates." Though I have little personal experience with Technology learning, I know many moms who use it and *rave* about it. (I've used Teaching Textbooks for math, and can see the wonder of it.)

The main argument against technology learning is that it can be expensive initially. If you opt for the online version, it can be an ongoing expense with each student. The exception to the price problem is to enroll in k12 through your local public school system. If you decide go that route, be aware that while the curriculum may be free (depending on your state), you may be completely under the control of the local school district as to scheduling and curriculum. If you have a special needs student that could be a bonus as you would have access to special education professionals. However, if one of the things that drew you to homeschooling was that you could tailor the lessons to your individual students, this may not be the best choice for you.

If you like the idea of technology learning and like the idea of not having to go-it-alone, there are a number of curriculum providers and distance learning academies such as Mother of Divine Grace, Homeschool Connection, and Fisher More Academy that offer technology learning as an option.

How do you choose the right curriculum that's best for you as a teacher, your lifestyle, and for your kids' learning style? And how do you know what it should be before you even start teaching?

I know. It's slightly insane, isn't it? A mom who's never taught before is supposed to somehow magically know what style of teaching and learning work best for her household without even having held a single book. It seems completely impossible. There's a reason for that. *It is*. While you can find pretty thorough descriptions on line, and even get help over the phone, it would be so much better if you could actually put your hands on the books.

If there are homeschooling groups in your area, contact them and see if they are planning a curriculum fair. These usually take place in the summer so as to allow parents the time to order any books they decide that they like. Most metropolitan areas will have some kind of curriculum expo each year.

If you live in the South, Mardel's Christian Bookstores carry a staggering selection of homeschooling books in their educational section. Take a mommy field trip and look around. They also have a great return policy, so that if you don't like something you're not stuck with it. (Save your receipts!)

Check your church bulletin and see if there is a homeschool support group or a parish liaison you could contact. Most people who have done this for a while have amassed a large collection of different curricula. Even if your contact doesn't have the particular grade you need, you can look at the books she does have and get a feel for the publishers' styles.

Check out your library. They won't have eighth grade math books, but if you're teaching lower grades, they will have some of the standards such as *Teach Your Child to Read in 100 Easy Lessons,* and *The Original Homeschooling Series* by Charlotte Mason. Ask your librarian for advice. (You're going to get to be good friends with her; you might as well go ahead and meet her now.) Check some things out and get a feel for the language and terminology. Educate yourself on the different styles of education available to you.

Do a couple test runs with your child, and see how they feel to you. Are you more comfortable with a formal school approach or are you naturally more playful? Your basic temperament and comfort levels are some of the most important things you are going to discover about yourself when it comes to teaching. You need to be willing to do what comes naturally to you.

Are there any particular places you go for curricula or do you just Google "homeschool curriculum" and sort through what pops up? Do you have any resources you've found helpful?

You can certainly Google homeschool curriculum. I did and got 2,070,000 results. That's way too much to sort through in one lifetime.

Conventions can be an amazing place to actually see, touch, and flip through curricula (and there are almost always convention discounts) and to educate yourself on the possibilities. Before you pay the registration fees, make sure to find out who's hosting the convention. A local homeschooling group's convention is a great thing. Conventions hosted by a particular curriculum provider can often turn into three-day infomercials for their products. They're great if you already know that you want what they're selling, but if you're looking for a wide variety of products to compare side-by-side, then be mindful of the fact that the competition probably won't be there.

If you are already familiar with curriculum providers and have a short list of those you are interested in knowing more about, check out their websites. Many will offer a discount for buying directly from the publisher. For almost everything else, I'd go to Rainbow Resource (rainbowresource.com). If you don't like to spend hours reading catalogs online (I hate it!), you can call and request their catalog. RR is the largest and best known clearing house for home education materials. The beauty of their company is that every item they sell has a clearly written description and review. Their reviews will let you know if teacher materials are included and for which courses they are necessary and on which you can save that money for something fun. Catholics will need to go elsewhere for catechism books. I recommend All Catholic Books (acbooks.net), Ignatius Press (ignatius.com), or Adoremus Books (adoremusbooks.com).

There is not yet one general place to go buy or compare all the Catholic curricula. Start at the curriculum websites – Seton Home Study (setonhome.org), Mother of Divine Grace (motherofdivinegrace.org), Catholic Heritage Curriculum (catholichomeschooling.com), St Thomas Aquinas Academy (staa-homeschool.com), Kolbe Academy (Kolbe.org), and Angelicum Academy (angelicum.net). Some of them sell their own curriculum, and others will point you in the direction of the best place to purchase the books they recommend. Poke around their sites and see which ones attract you. Ask the people you know in real life and the ones you find online for suggestions. You're going to have to do a little bit of digging and a fair amount of research if you want a Catholic education for your children, but it's definitely worth it.

When you choose curricula, do you find it best to pick one publisher and use their materials for all your classes, or do you pick one for each subject?

This is truly a personal preference issue. Many first time homeschoolers appreciate the ease of ordering a boxed curriculum, since: all the books and materials you need for the year come in a set. It takes the guesswork out of ordering. Box sets allow you to find your feet while making sure that you don't miss anything. There is an ease to it whether you choose Seton, Catholic Heritage, or one of the many Protestant or secular curriculum curricula.

I'm not that girl. I like to take it and tweak the things I like. Many curricula offerings, such as Mother of Divine Grace, make that very easy to do. After twelve years of teaching, there are some books I just like better than others. I've never found a single curriculum which has all of my favorites, so for now I'm cobbling my own together right up through high school.

Whether or not you should or could do this depends on you and on the state in which you live. We feel very fortunate to have lived in Oklahoma, and now in Texas, where the government leaves us alone and allows us to raise and educate our children as we deem best. We have never had to deal with oversight of any kind. If you are lucky enough to live in such a state, it's all up to you what you want to do. Some of the higher regulation states require that you submit your curriculum for approval before you are allowed to begin teaching your children. In those states, it might be easier to get an approval for something with which the inspector is already familiar or which has already been approved in that state. But to get a feel for things in your neck of the woods, check with your local resources. Call your town's homeschool groups, check on the HSLDA (Home School Legal Defense Association) website, and ask around before you venture too far off the beaten path.

Do the textbooks come with lesson plans?

Some do and some don't. Most boxed curricula will either include lesson plans or have them available for purchase. If you buy teacher's manuals, most of them will have lesson planning tips and often a script to follow in the margins. If you feel you need the extra help, then spend the money for them. When my children are in elementary school, I only splurge on them for math and foreign languages. I feel pretty confident in my ability to figure out the rest. In the upper grades, I go ahead and buy them. Distance learning academies also provide lesson plans with what they offer enrolled families.

Do you find that the same curriculum works for all your kids or do you pick up different materials for each one?

Many families are able to take a single curriculum and figure out a way to make it work for everyone. It may take some tweaking to make what works for the child who loves to read is also effective for teaching the child who hates it. So, while you can make the same books work, the way you use them will vary from child to child. On the other hand, many homeschooling families use different books or curricula for each child. These families have discovered that a cookie-cutter approach just isn't for them. It's really a personal and family preference issue.

Whatever way you decide to do it, keep in mind that kids are different and so it's only natural that their lessons will be different too. For instance, I have a son who loves worksheets in a way which I am convinced is unhealthy. His little brother would be near suicidal if I gave him the same workload. They are unique individuals and I've adapted what they are doing to match their learning styles. I know it sounds intimidating to say that, because how will you know what to adapt? It just *sounds* scary. You do it already in other areas of their lives. You will quickly figure out which boy can spend the day filling in the blanks and which one does better if you read him the page and let him answer you orally.

Give yourself a few weeks to be "Not-yet-the-expert." You really don't have to know it all on day one. You won't mess it all up that quickly.

I've decided on a boxed curriculum but don't love everything in it. How much latitude do I have to change things?

If you have decided to enroll in a learning academy such as Seton, k12, or Kolbe, the parent school will choose most of the curricula for you. The texts and add-ons for each subject are standardized for the ease of the parent at home as well as the teachers and staff in the office. The curriculum can be changed, with approval and guidance, to meet the special needs of the learning disabled and occasionally for parental preference. Some schools are more flexible than others. If it's important to you to be in charge, ask the school how much latitude they allow parents to have before you enroll for the year.

If you are an independent homeschooler, meaning that you have not enrolled in a learning academy but are using the books from a specific provider, then you have the freedom to choose whatever materials you want.

Are there some areas and subjects that overlap and my kids can share? How do you know?

Yes! They absolutely can overlap and share books and subjects, and I rejoice when that happens. It means that I can do half the planning for the same amount of learning. It's a 2 for 1 deal (or better.) When the students are close in grade and age you will find combining them on certain subjects easy to do. The subjects that overlap easily can best be described as anything with a story, i.e. literature, history, and even science. In the younger grades, these subjects do not require any particular skill level except listening or reading, and then doing the worksheets or activities that go with that lesson. So, you simply adjust, when necessary, the activity to the grade level of the students. For example, if you are teaching about the Revolutionary War, your third grader can do a crossword puzzle or definitions of vocabulary words and your first grader can color a picture of George Washington.

If you have an older child, you might still be able to arrange some overlap. My eldest, who is a high school junior, teaches reading to her 5-year-old brother. It counts as a reading class for him and towards a credit in child development for her. She could dissect a frog for science class, and her siblings, who are also studying frogs, could watch and offer color commentary on the entire operation.

How long does it take you to pick curricula? Is this something I need to start mid-summer, or before we end the previous year, or can we wait until a month before we start?

I am always in the process of picking new curricula. When I come across books, websites, or new resources, I bookmark them to research when I have the time. I begin researching in earnest every year around March or April. Homeschool conventions typically take place March-July, and I want to have a "shopping list" ready of things I want to see in person.

Post-convention (I don't go every year, just when there are things I want to examine before buying, or speakers I really want to hear), I begin ordering books in May or June. Most booksellers will have the books to you in a couple weeks; however, sometimes it can take a month or more. I don't

want to have to start school in September without all the books I need. Due to the higher order volumes in late summer, I have found it a good idea to call some of the smaller companies before I order to make sure what I want is in stock. A few times, I waited while my books were back-ordered for months only to have my order canceled completely the week after we'd started school. It creates havoc with my planning and is just generally uncool.

Although the curriculum research and discovery phase is never really going to end, at some point you just have to make a decision and go with it. Order your books in late Spring or early Summer to get any convention discounts, but don't put it off until August unless you want to start the year a book or two short.

What is the ballpark price for materials? Does it change with the child's age?

It can vary wildly. While some folks spend almost nothing and rely on books and materials from the library, others spend well in excess of $2,000 per year on each student.

One option at the less expensive end of the spectrum is k12, an online curriculum that in many states can be obtained for free through the school district – though with strings attached. Another low-cost option can be designing your own curriculum relying heavily on books that are available for free at your local library. That's not the easiest route to take, nor is it one for the faint of heart. If the books you need have been checked out by another patron, your plans are going to have to change on the spot, but if you are very determined and/or on a very tight budget, this may be the way to go.

Most beginning homeschoolers opt for a pre-packaged or box curriculum set, because it seems like a simple solution that will ensure everything's covered. The cost of these sets varies. Some provide only textbooks and lesson plans while others include online classes with live teachers. Naturally, the more bells and whistles there are the more you will pay. The basic sets begin around $250 (Catholic Heritage Curriculum, St Thomas Aquinas Academy) and top out around $1000 (Kolbe, Seton)

Homeschooling moms who cobble their own curricula together with textbooks they have hand-picked exercise greater control over their costs than those who choose a box curriculum set. Their spending for textbooks averages around $100-$200 per student for Pre K and Kindergarten, between $300-400 for Elementary and Middle School/Junior High, and $500+ for High School.

At this point in my family's homeschooling journey, it is rare for me to spend more than $600/year total for books and supplies because we re-use them, and that's for 5 students! When we add on co-ops and classes, we end up around $2,000 total. That's less than the cost of sending one child to private school for the year.

What is the purpose of writing a lesson plan, and do I need one?

The purpose of a lesson plan is for organization. Mine is my back-up brain written down to make sure that I don't miss anything, and so that I remember to do the fun things like art projects and not just the boring stuff. Whether or not you need one really depends on you. There are some amazing people who do better on the fly. They are at the top of their game when they wing it. That's not me, and would make me a lunatic. I need a plan written down on paper for each child. It helps me to keep track of where we are, and gives my children a measure of independence. My kids know where their schedules are, and on the days when life interrupts my perfect planning and my hair is on fire, they can pull out their books and just check things off as they do them.

How far in advance do you write one?

My personal plans extend a month out in broad planning and two weeks in specifics. Way out in advance, I write down field trips, science experiments that require planning, play dates, and anything else that will affect the schedule. I fill in the page numbers, test dates, and other details in two week blocks. I've done them further out, but something always seems to come up that requires rescheduling. Since I don't want to have to rewrite months of detailed plans, I no longer plan the nitty-gritty that far in advance. Here is what my schedule will look like a month or more out:

<u>December</u>

Math – Chapters 11-14

Literature – *Tom Sawyer*

History – *D'Aulaires' Book of Greek Myths* & *Famous Men of Greece*

Spelling – words ending in –ine and –ion

Religion – *Faith &Life* Chapters 9–11

Science – Anatomy

See how vague it is? That's all the planning I can do far in advance. When it gets closer, my daily plan will look like:

Tuesday December 14

Math – Page 115 even number problems & study for chapter review

Literature – read *Tom Sawyer* Chapter 8

History – Read Perseus and Medusa in D'Aulaire's. Summarize and illustrate for notebook. Read Socrates and place him on timeline

Spelling – Write definitions of spelling words from the list ending in –ion.

Religion – Read chapter 10 and answer chapter 10 essay questions in workbook

Science – Read chapter 12 on human anatomy. Copy skeleton diagram from page 69 of the workbook and label the major bones in the human body.

With a detailed plan such as this, I don't have to be on top of my older children as they are working. The written plan allows them the autonomy that they crave, and it helps to foster in them the sense of responsibility that they need.

What's the best way to write them out?

There are some moms who like to plan on the fly and just work their way through the books a section at a time. As they reach things that spark their kids' curiosity, they go looking for supplemental videos and books for enrichment.

Other moms prefer the old-fashioned pencil and paper method. Whether they choose a notebook, loose leaf paper, or a traditional teacher's lesson planner, there is something very satisfying about actually writing it down. I happen to love this method because it means I can rip the pages out and start over as often as I need to do it. The problem I've run into, however, is that I then have to store all those notebooks somewhere or I lose all the work I've done.

Which leads me to doing it on the computer. There are websites galore with free downloadable forms, and even more that charge for the use of theirs. You can spend hours looking at the different styles and ways of organizing your plans. I've never found one I like better than the others, and certainly not enough to pay for it, but I do like using a word processing program such as Microsoft Word. I pull up its calendar template and fill in the schedule in color-coded glory. (Don't judge.) I like being able to look at the page and think "Green is science". Play around with the free templates. Use what you have. There is no right or wrong, and absolutely no reason to pay for something you can get for free. (Unless you like one of the paid ones better. It's your money; just know that you don't have to invest it here.)

How rigidly do you stick to your plans? When do you deviate from them?

This is another one of those personal preference things. I'm not a rigid planner at all. It's not uncommon for us to change our plans abruptly when something cool comes up. Last year when the ducks at the neighborhood lake took their ducklings out to swim for the first time, the little kids and I spent the morning watching the mamas leading their babies to the water. We sat on the banks and read *Make Way for Ducklings*, and then the children drew pictures of it all in their science notebooks. It was infinitely more enjoyable than the lesson I had planned, and I was grateful that we were flexible enough to be able to go when my neighbor called and told me about them.

A friend of mine is the opposite. She is a planner and goes a bit mad if her schedule is upset. When we called her about the ducks, she checked her schedule and found a place in it the following week for a trip to the pond. The ducklings were still fuzzy cuteness when her family went and she didn't have to shift anything around to get there.

Neither method is better than the other; it's just the way we are built. She likes to know what's happening in advance and I like to be surprised by my day every now and again.

Luckily, we both have children who thrive with the mothers they were given.

To what extent can I re-use lesson plans? I'd like to only have to work this out once.

You can absolutely re-use them provided your children work at the same speed. If one is a faster learner though, you may have to speed up the planning or add in additional activities to keep up with his brain. If he is a bit slower you may have to spread the lesson out or remove activities so as not to overwhelm him. What you *will* be able to re-use are the lists of books and activities that go together so that you won't have to figure that out more than once. For example, while studying Ancient Egypt with your third grader, you'll remember to use the website salariya.com/web_books/mummy; to take a trip to the local museum to look at canopic jars; to make Egyptian amulets out of clay; and to read the book *Hatshepsut, His Majesty, Herself*. That's all good stuff that took me forever to compile. I would hate to have to remember all of that from one sixth grader to the next. I save lists of books and websites, templates of plans, and email short notes to myself. Keep everything you can if it helps you, but make sure it's somewhere that you can find it.

Have you ever gotten into the school year and discovered the books you had chosen weren't going to work out after all?

Absolutely. This happens to everyone at least once. It happens around here at least once every couple of years. There are years where it happens every few months. While it's not unheard of, it's also not that common. When is does happen it's usually in just one or two subjects and not all of them.

When something isn't working, do you have to buy a new curriculum and start from the beginning of it? Can you jump into the middle of the new book?

It depends what subject it is and how badly it wasn't working. If he just doesn't like it and seems a bit confused by the material, can you simply slow down and take a bit more time? You may just need to do a better job of explaining the material. In this case, a new curriculum isn't necessary at all, only a new teaching approach from you.

If he's totally lost then you should ditch the old stuff right away. Sell it on eBay and get him something new. If he's really clueless, then you need to start over at the beginning. Don't panic about how long it will take. I've been in this position before. It stinks, but you just double up lessons until you catch up to where you need to be. I've had my kids doing 5-10 lessons a day, flying through the stuff they understand, until we get to the place where they were lost. There really is no way to skip ahead, especially if it's math, in a new book. If it's an elective (such as a foreign language) and the year is more than half over, you might want to consider dropping it altogether and beginning fresh next school year.

As much as we sweat out our curriculum choices and worry whether the decisions we've made are the right ones, in the end it's not about the books. It's about our children discovering a love of learning and awakening their natural curiosity. As homeschoolers, our goal shouldn't be to cram as many facts into their heads as they can possibly remember; it should be to teach them to go looking for information, to make sense of the facts they find, and always seek to know more.

SIX

What Do I Really Need?

It is paradoxical that many educators and parents still differentiate between a time for learning and a time for play without seeing the vital connection between them." – Leo F. Buscaglia

Where does it all happen – do I need a classroom?

Do you need a classroom in order to teach your students? Will it be worthwhile to clear the furniture out of the formal dining room and start tacking the ABC's on the wall?

Maybe.

It all depends on what kind of teacher you are and what kind of space you have at your disposal. If you're living in an apartment and don't see where you could possibly fit in desks, chairs, and a blackboard, relax. You'll be fine in the space you have. If you like the relaxed feeling of curling up on the couch with your kids to read, are not the world's most organized person, and can't stand being in one room for extended periods of time you may want to hold off on setting up a miniature version of your first grade classroom. It just might not be your thing. On the other hand, if you're a person who thrives on order and neatness and want every space to have its own purpose *and* you have the room? You might want to think about figuring out which room to clear out, because *you* are a girl who needs a classroom. You should start planning for that.

Bottom line: a classroom can be a great luxury for the mom who thrives in a structured and organized environment, but if you're like me and only dream of structured and organized, it can become a waste of space in your household.

The truth is that most children want to be near mom. We all know this, both instinctively and from experience. Just step outside on the front porch to make a phone call and see how quickly every child in the house suddenly needs to join you out there. Are a few still inside? Make a move out of their line of sight and every little face in the house will be smushed up against the window to keep an eye on you. Living with small children is a little like being a celebrity trying to outrun the paparazzi. That's totally okay. They're supposed to like you that much – it means you've done something right. It is precisely because of this that we no longer have a classroom in our house.

For years, I created perfect study spots in our household. I painted the walls, made bulletin boards, hung educational posters, and did all I could to recreate a school atmosphere in the middle of what should have been our formal living room. We would use it for a month or two and then inevitably move back to the kitchen and family room. It wasn't the kids who hated it, I did. When I stopped trying to be the perfect mom and was honest about who I am (which you should always be or this will be way too hard), I realized that being cooped up in one place watching children learn made me insane. Maybe it was the mountain of laundry that called my name, but I couldn't just sit still all day. I needed to get up and move. Guess what? The children followed me. They didn't need a special room because I didn't need it. What works in our house is that I go about my day doing the laundry, washing the kitchen counters, and scrubbing the bathrooms while my children sit at the kitchen or coffee tables. They lounge and learn while I click my way through my to-do list. I'm always right there to answer questions, explain concepts, or just listen while they read, but I no longer feel like a prisoner.

One of my closest friends wants to cry when she hears how we do school. The very idea of my lack of structured space and formal organization stresses her out. Can you imagine if she had to live with our system at her house? We'd be peeling her off the ceiling every single day. Her classroom reminds me of the ones I knew as a student at St Gertrude's Catholic School a thousand years ago. Her students' desks are lined up in two neat rows. (She has 9 children, so there are quite a few desks to arrange.) Her big teacher's desk is at the front of the room facing her pupils. Her walls have a white board, Saint pictures, and maps. It looks like exactly what it is, a place for learning. She knew right from the beginning that she was a girl who liked structure, and her whole family is thriving and doing school at home in a room specially outfitted for that purpose.

Here are some things to think about before you invest the time and money to create a classroom in your house:

- Do you have space for one?
- If you have a room you can use, will you be using it for something else too? Is your school stuff going to get in the way of that something else?
- Can you afford to create a classroom? It's not absolutely necessary, so if your budget is tight, it might be better to spend it on better books or resources. If you can't, but you want one, why not piece it together a bit at a time? There's no rule that it has to be perfect by September.
- Look around your house. Are you an organization queen, or a bit more lax? If you need to have things in their assigned places, you might be really happy having a classroom. If you're more of a go-with-the-flow kind of girl, you might want to wait until you've actually taught for a month or two before you make a decision. (Don't let the cute ideas on Pinterest sway you on this. They almost get me every time.)
- Can you sit still? Are you capable of spending many hours in the same room? If you can't, you may not be thrilled at sitting behind a teacher's desk for hours at a time.
- Do your children thrive on or require structure? A separate designated space can help a lot of children transition between regular life and school time.
- Do you have high school students who need a quiet retreat from the noise of younger siblings? Algebra is hard enough without having to do it while

attempting to ignore your little brother. If your older kids share a bedroom with younger siblings, do they have a quiet place to go and learn? Do they need one?

- If you have very small children, how will they react to being cooped up in a single room all morning while the bigger kids do their schoolwork? Do you have things they can do to keep them occupied and quiet, or would you all be happier if they were running free-range around a larger area?

- Do you really want one? Do you dream about it at night and pick out paint colors during the day? If so, and you can, then please go for it! The most successful homeschooling will happen when mom is happy and settled in her space. If a classroom would make it better for you, then you should absolutely have one!

What is it that I really need?

- ***You need a table, desk, or other hard surface where children can sit and write.*** Kitchen counters with barstools are great for some children; others prefer a lap desk and a comfy couch. You don't need to go and buy anything at first, and maybe not ever. Watch your children for the first few weeks and see where they naturally gravitate. They will find what works for them. If you're a mom who needs order and things just so, then don't let them figure it out – get them a desk!

- ***Your students will need a place to read.*** Do you want this to happen at their desks, tables, or wherever they do their written school work? Keep in mind that a struggling reader may be embarrassed to sound out her lessons in front of a brother who just might laugh. (My children never laugh at each other. Nope. Never.) Our older children are allowed to take long reading lessons up to their rooms to escape the noise of the littles. They can go curl up on my bed if there is a reason their own rooms aren't an option, reasons like "naptime for your brother" or "you don't leave the Legos alone if you're out of my sight." We have done reading lessons curled up in dad's chair, or under the tree in the front yard. It all works, and can work well, but you need a place to read, and it needs to be a place where they are comfortable.

- ***The school books will need a home.*** Whether they live on the shelf in the classroom or on a bookshelf in your living room, school books need a place separate from the other books in your house. It doesn't have to be a shelf. A plastic tote where the books are piled when the work is done can work. Even if the only divider you have is a book end, there needs to be a boundary between the school books and the not-school books. Without something between them, they get mixed together, and you are going to spend many hours every week trying to figure out where the school books are.

- ***You need pencils.*** You are going to need three times as many pencils as you think you need. You are going to need your stash, your secret stash, and your backup secret stash. I don't know why you need so many pencils; I just know that I've never met a homeschool family who has enough. Even if you buy every pencil in the office supply store in August, you'll still be out by January. Buy pencils.

- ***Buy a pencil sharpener.*** Makes sense, right? If you need a plethora of pencils, you're going to need a way to make them useful. Don't cheap out on this. The little handheld plastic do-hickey that cost a dollar will last you three days max before it breaks, gets lost, or becomes part of an artistic masterpiece. Buy the good kind. A pencil sharpener is an investment worth making. The old fashioned hand crank kind will last forever, plus there's something satisfying in the sound of it. If you get an electric one, get the sort that plugs into the wall so that it can't walk away (I don't know where they all go, but I hope they are there together.) The electric ones are great for getting absolutely perfect super sharp points. If that matters to you or your students, go electric! It's also worth considering a separate sharpener for colored pencils. They will absolutely destroy your regular sharpener. There's just something about that colored lead that gums up the works.

- ***A copier/printer will make your life so much easier.*** When I began homeschooling, I bought workbooks and let my eldest use them. I had three small children and had no idea that the books I loved could go out of print or that the expense of new workbooks every year could be prohibitive. I also didn't know that there were times when we would need to do the same page more than once. We now make copies of everything. It has made homeschooling significantly less expensive and much easier. The same thing with the printer part of it. We print things daily from on-line for the littles. (There is no need to buy a coloring book. Just Google "coloring pages" and print the ones you want.) I also find that grading papers which have been printed out, instead of copied out long-hand, is easier for me to do, and easier for them to see my corrections. A good printer/copier combo is worth investing in when you have the money for it.

- *You need somewhere to put all those papers.* Homeschooled students generate mountains of papers that seem to pile up on every available surface. You need somewhere for the papers to go before you are buried alive. The best method I've found for storage and record keeping is a three part process: 1) I store all the work for the year as the children complete it in three ring binders – one for each subject. The years that I'm really on the ball, I put dividers in for each month so that I can easily find what I need. This is especially helpful if you have to turn in samples to your county or curriculum provider. 2) At the end of the month, I scan in anything I might possibly need for later reference and store it on a flash drive or online back-up service. 3) Then, and this is just my own personal preference, I keep hard copies of the important stuff, anything I might need for a review or just the work that I really love, for a year before I throw them away. So, let's review that one – *you need a three-hole punch, binders, a scanner, a flash drive, and a trash can.* You could even skip the middle steps and put the *binders* in a *box* for a year before *throwing them away.*

- **You're gonna need some art supplies.** Lots of them. Stock up at the back-to-school sales when you can get crayons for a quarter. Buy tons of crayons. We also stock up on construction paper, scissors, water colors, glitter, glue, and glue sticks. Figure out how you really feel about markers before you let that evil into your house. I know moms who have never had a marker issue ever. I'm not them. My little angels colored the sleeping baby's face to look like a clown while I was moving the laundry. (Did I mention that it was the same day we were supposed to get family pictures taken?) They may say "washable" on the package, but that green just wouldn't come all the way off his nose. We no longer do markers. We don't do play dough either since I spent an afternoon cleaning it off the dog. Figure out your own level of mess-tolerance and, balance it with the kids' need to create. Then organize the art stuff you allow in a place where your students can see what's available. I have mine hanging on the inside of the kitchen pantry door in one of those hanging shoe bag contraptions, the kind with all the pockets. We can all see what we've got, but keeping it in the kitchen means that I have control of access, and there's a sink nearby in case of emergencies.
- **With all this artwork, you're going to need a display place.** The front of your refrigerator is

going to fill up quickly, and if you have more than one artist, they will jockey for "the good spots." The way to keep the peace is to have a place for each artist's masterpieces to go. While I love the idea of a bulletin board, or even wall space designated for the children's artwork, I have 7 children and the walls fill up quickly. So, we've given each child a cabinet door in the kitchen. I can't handle the clutter or papers hanging all over my kitchen, so they get the *inside* of their cabinet doors unless the work is truly spectacular in which case it gets framed and hung on a wall. After a week of viewing, all artwork moves to three ring binders for each child. At the end of the year, we keep what we love and toss the also-rans. I know it sounds mean to throw their stuff away. I thought so, too, way back in the beginning. But once I saw the volume of pictures that one 7-year-old girl can make in a single afternoon, I changed my tune pretty fast.

If you could have anything you want, what would you have?

In a perfect world, what would I have? I love that kind of question. Here what's on my wish-list:

- *I would love to have a computer or even computers just for school.* A lot of time goes to waste in my household in waiting for the computer. I use it for writing and household management, my children use it for research and language lessons, and we all use it for play. That's a lot of use in one piece of equipment. In a perfect world, we'd have at least two and probably three just for school. This isn't a perfect world. We're saving our pennies for one.

- ***I would LOVE to have a bigger copier.*** I splurged last year and bought a better copier/printer that can do stacks of pages at a time. I love it! In my dream world, I have one that collates and staples the pages for me. I keep an eye on Craigslist for a deal on a used one, but I'm not really committed to the idea. I'm not sure where I would put it.

- ***I dream of owning a microscope.*** I really want the cool kind that hooks up to the computer so that we could all look at the images together. (My super-awesome just-for-school computer, of course!) I imagine us looking at amoebas from the creek by our house, or studying the cellular structure of... cells, I guess. I know the reality would be different and my sons would be looking at the physical properties of boogers, but I don't care. I really want a microscope.

- ***I wish I could have the Beast's library.*** You know the kind on *Beauty and the Beast*? He gave it to Belle as a gift. That was the dreamiest part of the movie for me. I love books. I would get rid of the trash books (all those stupid movie tie-in books – I wince every time someone toddles up to me with one in hand) and fill my house to the rafters with classics if I could. I love the idea of what that would do for my children.

- ***I want locked cabinets for art supplies and spare wall area to put them.*** Finger paints are controlled substances and need to be under lock and key. Glitter is like crack to my 8-year-old. She's a serious addict. Then there's the boy who I'm pretty sure would eat paste if I weren't looking. Art supplies are a serious addiction around here. They need a lock and key to keep them safe.
- ***In a perfect world I would have a bright yellow Corvette.*** What? Don't judge. If it's yellow it totally counts as a school bus. You dream about the school supplies you want, and I'll imagine mine.

The list of things you will need in order to homeschool your children is unique to your own family. It will depend on your family's personalities, preferences, space, budget, and curriculum requirements. I have seen families educate on a shoestring – getting books from the library, printables from online, and copying their work by hand into spiral notebooks, and I've seen families who spend a small fortune – building a custom classroom, purchasing expensive curricula, and buying top-of-the-line computers and science equipment. What I have *not* seen is a direct relationship between what parents have spent on teaching them and results. The biggest determining factors for academic success seem to be consistency – getting up and working every day, and the enthusiasm of the teacher for both the subjects and her pupils. Money can't buy either one of those. Invest money in the things that give you the confidence to be able to teach, and in what will interest your children in learning. The rest of it is just window dressing – except for that pencil thing. I was totally serious about   that.

SEVEN

Learning Styles

"Knowledge which is acquired under compulsion has no hold on the mind. Therefore do not use compulsion, but let early education be rather a sort of amusement; this will better enable you to find out the natural bent of the child." –Plato

You mentioned learning styles in the last chapter. What are the different basic learning styles and what do they look like?

The basic learning styles fall under three different umbrellas. These are: visual – learn best by seeing and reading; auditory – learn best by hearing and listening; and kinesthetic – learn best by doing or while their bodies are in motion. It is important to remember that while we all have a preference for one learning style or another, most people are a combination of all three to varying degrees.

Visual learners are the kids most schools are designed to teach. While all students process information through their eyes, these students *prefer* to access it this way. They thrive in a world of books and flow charts. The more visually stimulating information is, the happier they are.

Auditory learners like language and sound. Sometimes they like to listen, and sometimes they like to talk. These students are often your chatterboxes, if for no reason other than to hear the sound of their own voices. (You've said, "I think he talks just to hear himself speak." You were right!) The chatter might drive you insane, but it makes his brain happy. They have good memories and will be able to recall every detail of what you said long after you've forgotten saying it.

Kinesthetic learners are the bodies in motion. They need to be moving for their brains to even turn on! They are often misunderstood as being hyperactive, but don't be fooled! These students remember things they do after doing them just once. They like to act things out or do things "hands on." These kids climb, run, jump, and never seem to stop. Have you ever forgotten something , gotten up, begun to walk away, only to have the information pop into your head? Your body in motion turned your brain on! That's life for a kinesthetic learner. Physical activity means brain stimulation, so keep them going and they'll learn even faster.

Hmmm... can you give an example of how you would teach the same lesson to each kind of learner?

Let's pretend that we're going to teach a second grader about the life cycle of frogs.

With my visual learner, we would begin with a trip to the library for books with lots of pictures such as *The Life Cycle of a Frog* by Bobbie Kalman. We'd cart those home along with any videos and easy readers on the subject. I would scour the internet to find lots of worksheets with pictures of eggs, tadpoles, and frogs for her to color. We might make a poster with cut-out pictures of every stage of a frog's life (Google – it's your friend. You can find more pictures of frogs than you've ever dreamed of wanting to find.) We would color, cut, draw, and paste to her heart's content.

For my auditory learner, I'd make a trip to the library for the same books, but I would either read them to her or have her read them out loud to me. *She needs to hear the words to remember them!* I'd find videos online such as the Discovery Channel Series *Life*'s episode on frogs (it's episode #2.) Make sure that whatever shows you find have *lots* of narration, but don't be dismayed if she isn't always looking at the screen. If the sound is on, she's paying attention. I would find any and all silly songs about frogs and sing them with her as we look at pictures, do worksheets, or attempt anything visual that doesn't come with its own sound track. When you're done reading the lesson or watching the show, have her narrate back to you what she's learned. (Narrate back is the fancy homeschooler way of saying "Have her tell you all about it.") "Hearing it" coming back out of her own mouth will reinforce everything she's learned.

With my kinesthetic learner, we'd go on a frog hunt! I would do a bit of research and find a nearby pond or creek with tadpoles swimming around. As we searched the shoreline for clutches of floating eggs and scanned the water for tadpoles, we could talk about how they look like fish but are really baby frogs. I'd help her try to catch tadpoles in a jar for closer inspection (bonus points if we can catch ones sprouting legs!), and maybe catch a frog or two. Hopefully I'd remember to bring hand wipes, as it's a guarantee that the frog will pee on someone – that's their defense mechanism... which gives me the perfect opening to talk about defense mechanisms in nature! Dogs catch the frog; the frog pees in his mouth; the dog lets him go. Boom! Science lesson learned. After we had walked and explored, we would curl up together on the couch (because kinesthetic learners don't do well in desks or at tables) and read *The Life Cycle of a Frog*. And I'd be ready for the many wiggly interruptions that were sure to come.

While the prospect of having to tailor every lesson to each child seems daunting, it doesn't have to be at all. Most children are flexible enough to learn and benefit from learning in a combination of styles. For example, you don't have to make *everything* hands on for your kinesthetic learner. He can stand while writing or make laps around the room as you read aloud. While it's helpful to know how each child learns best, especially when you're tackling a particularly difficult assignment, it isn't necessary for every single lesson. As important as their lessons are, learning to be adaptable and make things work for themselves are important things to learn as well.

If you have an auditory learner, how do you keep his out-loud learning from bothering everyone else?

That depends, are we talking about the noise of his lessons bothering others, or the noise of *him* bothering others?

If it's the sound of his lessons, there's really only one solution: headphones. Play music for him, let him listen to books on tape (are they still called that if they're MP3's?), or even YouTube videos with the sound turned up and the headphones on. He can sit happily at the same table as his siblings and do his work and no one else has to hear it.

If he's a chatterbox learner, you may have to separate him from everyone else or teach him at a different time if he can't be quiet. It's often hard to get auditory learners to *just stop talking*. For the sake of everyone else's sanity, he's going to have to learn self-control and you're the lucky mom who gets to teach it to him. (Hooray for you!) Don't fool yourself into thinking that there's a quick fix. It's going to take years and years for him to master the ability to control his mouth and not hum, talk, or sing while he's working. Although helping him figure out how to manage his natural tendencies is a big job, he's going to need to learn how to do it or he'll drive his co-workers batty someday.

If your kid is a heavily kinesthetic learner, how do you teach him to do things that you yourself don't know how to do?

You're either going to learn how to do those things, or you're going to get to watch the show as he figures it out for himself. You didn't have this child so that you could sit still, did you? Life is about learning new things, and as this kid's mom, you're going to learn all kinds of crazy new skills. Just embrace the challenge and run with it. Teaching him will be one of the most exciting things you will ever do. This is the learning adventure you will still be talking about when all your children have grown up and moved out of the house.

It's not going to be all catching frogs and building rockets. Kinesthetic learners don't just need to do things *to* learn, they need to do things *while* they learn. The easiest adjustment to make is to allow him to stand at the counter and do his school work instead of having him sit in a desk or chair. If he has to sit for your own peace of mind, then put him on a yoga ball so that he can bounce and roll a bit as he's working. You might give him a tennis ball to roll around with his foot or a squishy ball to play with in his hand. It doesn't have to be his whole body that's moving, but at least part of it will need to be if you want him to be able to think. You are right when you complain that he can't sit still. He can't if you want him to learn anything. This is the foot-jiggling, pencil-tapping, chair rocking kid who drove you crazy in school. Congratulations, he's now learning at your kitchen table. He's so lucky to be home with you. You get that he's not trying to bother his siblings; he's actually trying really hard to learn. (Okay, sometimes he's trying to bug his brother. I'm not gonna lie.)

How much do I need to know about learning styles just to get started?

Honestly? Not a whole lot much as they need to without bothering everyone else, you'll figure it out pretty quickly. You don't need to label your son as kinesthetic to know that he reads better when he's curled up on the couch than when he's sitting upright at a desk. It won't matter if you call your daughter an auditory learner as long as you recognize that she learns better when there' s music playing in the background. *Calling* your son a visual learner won't improve how you teach him. Simply let him draw the charts and diagrams he needs to help him remember things.

Understanding how different children learn is helpful to you as a teacher. Not only will it help you know how to approach each new student, but it will also help cut down on the "but your sister learned it this way with no problem" frustration. Knowing about learning styles will give you some starting points for how to teach your children and some cues to look for, but it all comes down to observing the children themselves. Fortunately, the person who knows them better than anyone in the world is now also their teacher.

The best thing you can do to accommodate your children's learning styles is to throw out the mental image of happy children sitting quietly around the kitchen table (or at their desks) doing their lessons. If you're lucky, you'll get one of that kid. But the rest of them will thrive too – when you give them the freedom and understanding to figure out how their own brains work best.

. If you pay attention to your children and give them the leeway to move, draw, or talk as

Can you recommend any beginner resources to me on the subject?

For a quick overview and fast reading, I really like these websites:

http://www.classroom-management-success.org/different-learning-styles.html

www.education.com/reference/article/childrens-learning-styles/

www.learningstyles.org

www.learning-styles-online.com/ includes an online assessment

If you prefer holding a book in your hands to reading on a computer screen, you can try:

The Big What Now Book of Learning Styles: A Fresh and Demystifying Approach by Carol Barnier

Talkers, Watchers, and Doers: Unlocking Your Child's Unique Learning Style by Cheri Fuller

Learning Styles: What Are They? How Can They Help? by Diane Lamarche-Bisson

EIGHT

Homeschooling with Different

Ages

A cross-eyed teacher can keep twice the number of children in order than any other, because the pupils do not know who she's looking at.
– Four Hundred Laughs: Or, Fun Without Vulgarity, compiled and edited by John R. Kemble, 1902

We've been thinking about doing this, but I just don't get how to handle the baby during "school". How do you do it?

It depends what age baby we're talking about here. When I have an infant, she is wherever she needs to be. Sometimes that is in bed asleep, nursing, sitting in my lap, being jiggled on my hip, crawling on the floor, or playing in the playpen. I've never had difficulty folding new babies into the routine of school, and my older children see babies as a part of life. They will usually continue working if I have to leave the room for a diaper change or to put the baby down for a nap.

Older babies are a bit more work because they like to be the center of attention and frequently (read ALL THE TIME) get into things and places they shouldn't. That's why I'm a big fan (huge!) of play-yards and safety gates. You will save yourself a lot of time if the littlest one is in a confined area that has been baby-proofed and is well equipped with non-electronic toys. (This is really so important as the tinny sounds of electronic noise will distract even the most dedicated student, so forget an 8-year-old boy being able to work with all that racket.)

I also make sure to schedule anything that is hands-on, messy, or requires all my attention for times when the baby is sleeping. Of course, this means that you have to be flexible about what time these projects will actually occur. The day you plan on the little one sleeping from 1-3 is the day he will opt for a morning nap. Do the project then!

If you are blessed, as I have been, with a youngest who can scale the walls of the baby gate, or just hates being put down, it's time to call in the older kids for help. The big kids love an excuse to take a mini-break in the middle of the day, and the baby loves someone new to play with. Even a 6 or 7-year-old can make goofy faces to keep the littlest one entertained. You don't need an all day break here, just windows of 20-30 minutes to do some one-on-one teaching. Big kids can be a great help if you just ask.

Key to homeschooling with a small child in the house is finding a place within yourself of calm-like Zen. Your day will never go as you planned it. That's important so I'm going to repeat it: y our day will *never* go as you planned it. Sometimes in good ways, like when the 7-year-old suddenly "clicks" on a math concept and does a week's worth of work in one hour, or in bad ways such as the day the 2-year-old threw up on the school books. (Figuring out how to get puke out of textbooks is its own kind of science experiment.)

Bottom line? Homeschooling with a baby requires adaptability and a sense of humor. Your children will learn great things from it. For instance, my eldest two can study almost anywhere in any kind of chaos. They've learned how to tune out distractions. (That should be a huge help in college.) My third has learned he can't tune out anything and that he has to be responsible enough to know when he's overwhelmed with outside commotion and remove himself to his room until the chaos calms down. And me? I've learned how to laugh in the midst of it all, and that occasional chaos doesn't make me a failure. This is a marathon not a sprint. The results are measured at the end of it all.

Okay, but what about with a preschooler?

Preschoolers are their own kind of wonderful, aren't they? They are curiosity, excitement, movement, and energy all rolled up into one little body that's constantly in motion. Unfortunately, what makes them amazing and wonderful is also what creates a challenge when you're trying to homeschool the older kids. If you're paying attention to the older kids that means no one is watching the 3-year-old. If no one watching the 3-year-old, there will be mayhem.

That's okay. It won't happen (too often) at your house because you're the girl with a plan. What preschoolers need to keep them safe, and not playing in the flour in the pantry, is a distraction. They need an activity to keep them out of trouble. My favorite one of these is a nap. If you are fortunate enough to have a preschooler who is still napping in the afternoons, this is the perfect time for schoolwork. It's easy to fall into the "school starts at 8:00 because that's what regular schools do" trap. They start at 8 because they have to. As a homeschooling parent, you get to be in charge of the schedule. No rules dictate the time at which you must teach your children. I find that the quiet lull of after lunch naptime is the perfect opportunity to go in depth with my bigs.

If your sweet one doesn't nap...I'm so sorry....then it's on to other strategies. I know that television is anathema to many, many homeschooling families, but hear me out here. TV in excess can be a bad thing, but if you control it, it can be a tool like any other. TV is invaluable for a 30 – 60 minute stretch of time when you need the littles to just be quiet. Times like testing, explaining Algebra, dissecting a frog, or any time when the help of a three-year-old is actually a bit less than helpful. Educational videos like LeapPad's Letter Factory or religious ones like Veggie Tales are great for keeping them quiet. I tell myself that it's not a total waste, because there is some value to what they're seeing.

Not convinced to turn on the TV, or have a little one who just won't watch it? Then you've got to get a bit more creative, or learn to Google. Better yet, use Pinterest to keep track of things to keep them busy. I have pins for quiet activities, outside stuff to do, and things for littles to make.

The hardest part is finding activities that don't require mom's absolute attention or supervision. Here are a few that work for us just to give you an idea of what you're looking for:

- I put pipe cleaners in the holes of my colander and then gave it to the 3-year-old. "What do you think it is?" I asked him. He replied that it was an alien hat and wore it around for a while. When he finished conquering the universe of my kitchen, he pulled them all out and then put them back in again. He bent the pipe cleaners around his wrist and then straightened them out again. The pipe cleaners and colander entertained him for close to an hour.

- I put the website phoebeallens.com on my laptop and let him watch the real-time live streaming of a hummingbird mama and her babies. It's ridiculous how fascinating he finds their little family. He will watch the birds for easily half an hour. The only warning is that it *is* real life. The day that the lizard came and ate one egg and the mom pushed the other out of the nest meant that I got to spend the afternoon discussing predators and instinct. It was educational, just not in a way I had planned for it to be.

- I've had them string Cheerios on a piece of yarn. This not only helps to develop fine motor skills, but if you roll it in peanut butter and then bird seed later, it makes a fine bird feeder. Hang the new birdfeeder near a window and let him watch everyone who comes to eat it.

- Coloring! It seems so easy and obvious that it almost feels like cheating, but it's not! Coloring books, coloring pages, blank paper for them to draw on: it makes the little guys feel like they're doing school, too, which means that your other kids may actually get to do a bit of school themselves.

There are literally thousands of activities you can set up for your littles to do to keep them occupied, quiet, and out of the flour (it really isn't pretty, but they seem fascinated with it. It's not only at my house, is it?). It will take a bit of practice, research, and planning on your part until you get a feel for what works with your own children.

When I was a new homeschooler, I felt like a failure because I couldn't come up with a list of these things off the top of my head. I can now see how silly that is. There are some moms who are gifted in that area and then there are the rest of us. We are the ones who shamelessly rip them off. Buy a book on preschool activities. Subscribe to Family Fun magazine. Use Google and Pinterest to abandon. It doesn't matter what you use, or where you get ideas, but arm yourself with a fun and fast diversion for the 3-year-old and keep your sanity for the hard stuff.

I'm not worried about the little kids. I just don't understand how I'm going to teach three different grades at the same time.

The key to schooling multiple ages and grade levels at once is timing. While I'll admit that it sounds nearly impossible to teach four grades of math at the same time (and I think it just may be), no one is asking you to do that. What seasoned homeschoolers will tell you is that you have to stagger it. I do math with my 12-year-old while the 8 and 11-year-olds do handwriting and the 5-year-old plays. Next is math with the 11-year-old while the 8 year old does her spelling words, the 12-year-old reads literature, and the 5-year-old writes his letters. It just continues on with one child doing a class that requires my attention while the others work independently nearby. I schedule the subjects that need supervision for the morning when we all have the energy and patience for it and end the day with art and music which require very little oversight from me at all.

I know several families who have solved this problem, especially in the case of special needs children, by staggering their start times. Early elementary grades take only an hour or two a day, so you can conceivably focus solely on one child and then the next while the other children play. A friend of ours teaches three children this way every morning, one at 8:00, one starting at 9:30, and the last from 10:30-lunch time. This leaves her the entire afternoon, when the youngest is napping, to concentrate on 7th grade with her eldest who has Asperger's.

Keep in mind, while trying to juggle the education of multiple children, there's no such thing as wrong or right. There is only what works and what doesn't. The fact that no rules exist for how to homeschool is what makes it both so simple and so frustratingly complex. No one says that dad can't do history with your children at night before bedtime, or that something's wrong with letting your night owl *begin* his school day at 6 p.m. if that works for you. You just have to be willing to keep trying, adapting, and tweaking until you figure out what's best for all of the people who live in your household.

P.S. That includes you, too.

What if I have an only child? How will that impact the way I teach her?

With an only child you may be tempted (I've seen it many times) to hover over her and not give her the space to learn things without mom's help. It's hard for moms of only children to step back and let them breathe a bit, but you have to make the effort. Your goal as a homeschooling parent should not be to ensure that she knows everything it is possible to know. You're not grooming her to show off on the Late Show (unless you are...you're not though...right?), you're raising her to be a successful adult. What does it mean to be a successful adult? That answer is different for every parent. Most of us would say that at least part of it is not depending on mom for every little thing. That has to start somewhere. Giving her the space to learn and make her own mistakes is a really good and safe place to begin.

Give your child the gift of teaching her how to learn. Allow her to read the material alone, let her search for the answers herself, give her space to discover the triumph of figuring something out and then getting to show it to you. You have to walk away if that's ever going to happen for her.

If you can't restrain your impulse to "help," then find something else to distract you while she's doing her school work. I find that folding laundry near where my children are learning allows them to ask me for help when necessary, but distracts me from over-assisting. It's the reason I began to blog on my laptop while my wee ones learned at the table next to me; even those of us with a thousand children will helicopter over them. I can't even imagine the temptation for a mom of one.

Teaching children at home is an adventure. Whether you have one child or twenty, it's an everyday juggling act balancing the dual responsibilities of teacher and Mom. It's hard to be the teacher who wants her to learn to do things on her own and the mom who wants her to get straight A's. On those days when you're unsure of which one she needs you to be, simply stop and pray for her. Then sit next to her and pray *with* her. Pray for the strength to allow her the space to grow up into her own strong woman, and that God will grant you the wisdom to know when you need to step in.

NINE

High School

"To bring up a child in the way he should go, travel that way yourself once in a while." – Josh Billings

High school is what gives me the jitters. Just the thought of Geometry proofs and I break out into a cold sweat. What is the Peloponnesian War? How am I ever going to be able to do it?

Are there really people on this planet who don't break into a cold sweat at the thought of doing Geometry proofs? I think I would go sit in the corner, rock and suck my thumb if I thought I ever had to do them again. I taught them last year anyway. You *can* do this.

First, keep this in mind if your children are still small and high school is years away: you are laying the foundations now for high school learning. The goal of homeschooling is *not* to cram information into our children's heads. No matter how many nose-y people quiz your kids, it's not about how good they look to the neighbors. The point of education is to teach children how to think critically and how to teach themselves. If you have done this well, they will be able to teach themselves Geometry. (Oh, Happy Day!) If they aren't mathematically inclined, you will have become so much better educated in Math (or History, Grammar, etc.) that, with the magic teacher's manual on your side, you will be able to tackle whatever subjects she studies. Rest assured that you won't have to conquer this alone. There are online courses, study groups, and co-ops out there for homeschoolers. In some states, your children can attend the local public schools for select classes, or you can hire/barter for tutoring. There are plenty of resources out there, but maybe you should tackle 2nd grade before you begin to stress over what you'll do when your now 7-year-old is a sophomore.

If you've already got a high school student and you're just beginning, I admire your bravery. You're jumping straight in to the deep end of the pool. Go you with your brave self!

I would begin this teaching adventure by being completely honest with my students. If the Peloponnesian War has you scratching your head and wondering where Peloponnesia is on the map (it was a war between Athens and Sparta – the Greeks), then tell your daughter that. Be frank with her about the fact that there are gaps in your own knowledge, and that this means the two of you will be learning Ancient History together. Then tackle it that way – learn it with her. You'll be the better for it, and she will get to witness the truth that learning takes a lifetime. There are few things more interesting or exciting than being a part of someone's great "Ah-Ha!" moment. Give your child the gift of discovering things with you. Let her witness your "Eureka!" moment. Your relationship will be so much stronger by the end of the year.

Look for ways that help you simplify the teaching. There are curriculum options, such as Teaching Textbooks, that offer interactive computer learning. Computer learning is great for the nervous or novice homeschool mom. Your child sits down at the computer and the program teaches her. If you know that you can't teach something, then get her something that will. Mother of Divine Grace, for example, has online classes through Adobe Connect. The public schools offer computer classes through k12. Homeschool Connections (homeschoolconnectionsonline.com) offers a full curriculum for junior high and high school students, or you can pick and choose the courses that you need. A quick Google search will lead you to a plethora of options. You should be able to find one that you feel comfortable using.

If computer learning doesn't appeal to you or isn't an option you can enroll in a co-op – either a formal private school model or an informal teaching swap with other parents. A co-op will not only help with the teaching, but it will also offer a social outlet for your child. Loosely defined, a co-op is a group of families who get together to share teaching and other duties. Most co-ops will offer math, lab science, at least one foreign language, and usually a writing program. A larger co-op will offer all the classes she will need for high school. It is generally one day of classroom instruction followed by four days of homework. Don't think you're getting off easy here. It is generally assumed that parents will be available at home to answer basic questions and do the grading. The individual teachers may be available to help with more difficult questions, but the bulk of the instruction will still fall on your shoulders.

In its purest form, a co-op is an even exchange of instruction for instruction. You teach biology; someone else teaches literature. Usually though, most co-ops are made up of teachers who charge a monthly or yearly fee for their classes. This can range from a nominal charge to $300 or more per class. Look around and find one that works for your family and budget. If you don't find one, you can always organize your own.

No co-ops or computer schooling? Call your local community college and find out about tutors. There are many, many college students who would jump at the chance to make some extra money tutoring your child. Call the department you want directly and ask them for a recommendation. I'm a little afraid of who might answer an ad you tack to the bulletin board, but if you're willing to try it you just might find a gem. While most tutors charge $20 an hour or more, many are willing to barter. I traded weekly home-made bread and cookies for voice lessons for my eldest, and found an education major who was thrilled to help our dyslexic son with his eye exercises in exchange for a home-cooked meal. Don't underestimate the power of home-baked goodies or pot roast!

Do you have a student who is ready for a bit more of a challenge? Why not enroll him in classes at the local community college? Most local colleges are welcoming to homeschooled high school students, especially juniors and seniors. The students will have to meet the basic acceptance requirements for the school including test scores, a transcript, and perhaps a personal interview. It's nothing too scary. The upside to taking classes at the community college is that your student may earn dual credits, toward high school graduation and college hours, for taking only a single class. Most states offer a dual credit or concurrent enrollment program through the local public school districts, and homeschooled students are eligible for these programs which cover most, if not all, of the tuition costs. You will still be responsible for books and fees, but that's still a pretty nice scholarship to start off your child's college career.

High school is daunting because it "counts" in ways the earlier grades do not. Pa rents sense that it is much more serious, and it is, but don't let that scare you. If you are willing to look around, ask some questions, be flexible, and completely honest, then you *can* teach it or find the help you need.

The thing that worries me about teaching high school is the hormonal roller coaster of a teenager. You have a high school student. Do her hormones ever make you want to send her off to boarding school?

Yes! A thousand times, Yes! There absolutely are days when I just don't want to deal with the mood swings or the tears any longer. The hormones can get out of control. That's not a homeschool thing. That's a life thing.

I try very hard to wait until it passes and then we sit down and discuss what's going on. Most of the time, my daughter knows she's being an out of control lunatic and she's even less happy about it than I am. We've talked very plainly about puberty and hormonal cycles. So much so that she is able to figure out what's going on in her own body. While I understand PMS lunacy, making the rest of the household miserable is *never* allowed. She's going to have to get a handle on her moods at some point in her life, and it's easier now while she's at home than it will be in college or out in the world. A meltdown in our home is bad. An explosion at work could be a career killer. It's better to help her figure it out now.

The key to living with teenagers is honesty and clarity. What *exactly* do you expect of her? What *exactly* does that look like? I have found that specificity helps. Don't accept a messy bedroom? You have to give them an example and definition of clean. I helped my daughter clean her room and then took a picture of it for her for a reference so that she knows *that's* what I call a clean room. If you have a curfew, be specific about what it is *before* your teen is asking to go out with friends; ditto for your family's rules on dating and opposite sex friendship/relationships. If you have high standards and expectations for academics, tell your children precisely what you need to see to keep you happy. Teenagers are brilliantly creative about getting into trouble, but need a step-by-step roadmap of what their parents expect of them. Don't leave her guessing. Lay it all out there. Write it down if you think you might need a reference at some point. Make her sign it if you think she's not paying attention.

Hormonal wonkiness in teenagers happens the same way tantrums happen in a 2-year-old. It's developmentally appropriate. (Sorry to have to be the one telling you that.)

Just like when your child was a terrible two, the terrible part isn't acceptable. Ever. It's your job to tell her that (or him...either way). Just because teenagers look almost adult doesn't mean that they're not still kids. They need you to be their parents just as much now as in the toddler years. It's only the challenges that have changed.

How do you handle college admissions? What if they want a transcript? Are there schools which require a GED?

In my experience, and that of the many homeschool families I know, it's not any more difficult for homeschool students to get into college than it is for other students. The school is going to want a transcript, so you will need to keep track of all classes and the grades earned. It doesn't hurt to print off a list of graduation requirements in your state and keep them somewhere handy. As you check off the required courses, your student will move ever closer to graduation. (Eek!)

I wrote out my daughter's transcript on a Word template called "Transcript". There were several different styles from which I could choose. I've heard nightmare stories about the detail and descriptions required of a homeschool transcript. Ours was fairly simple, and we've sent it out to several colleges and universities and have never been asked for elaboration. The admissions guy at our local college said that as long as the SAT or ACT test scores seem to align the grades you have recorded, they don't really need all of that detail.

If the keeping of grades and writing of a transcript is more than you feel up to doing, there are many curriculum providers who are happy to do it for you for a fee. Some of them provide the service automatically when you enroll your family in the program.

Should she take the GED? I can't see that it's really a bad idea, but I'm not convinced it's necessary either. Provided that your child is going to college and will graduate, a GED becomes irrelevant. If she's headed to trade school, or you don't think she's college material, a GED might be wise. It would be much easier for her to pass it at 18 than for her to try and pass it at 28. Do a little research and discuss it in your family. Like most issues in homeschooling, there is no one answer that suits everyone.

What about scholarships? Can homeschooled kids get National Merit Scholarships? Do they qualify for other kinds?

Not only do homeschooled students qualify for scholarships, many families count on them.

National Merit Scholarships are based upon the PSAT, a test taken in October of your student's junior year. Check the College Board website (www.sat.collegeboard.org/home) for the date and for local schools offering it. You may have to muscle your child into being allowed to sit for the test, but know that the rules are on your side. Any public school offering the test to its own students is required by the College Board to let your homeschooled child take it too.

This is one of those things worth fighting for. Better yet, let your son call and make the arrangements for himself. Being able to make arrangements and stand up for himself are important life skills. This is a great time to teach them.

As for other kinds of scholarships, homeschool students win a lot of money every single year. Our two favorite sites for lists and applications for various scholarships are www.fastweb.com and www.cappex.com. Apply. Apply. Apply. There is no reason not to fill out that paperwork. Get every penny you can. The scholarship people like homeschoolers.

Can they get career counseling from somewhere? I feel unqualified to introduce them to careers far outside my range of knowledge, and I would love for them to get to talk to someone they won't be rolling their eyes at about what might be a good fit for them.

Encourage your teenager to investigate any jobs he finds interesting and to contact people who have those jobs to talk about them. One of the opportunities homeschool students have that traditionally schooled students don't is that they can spend time during the day doing an internship or job shadowing. I'm continually amazed at how willing professional people are to show off what they do for a living, and to let a high school student follow them around. I know kids who have spent the day with a heart surgeon watching surgery from the observation room, assisted a jockey in putting the horses through their paces, interned in the accounting department of a Fortune 500 company, and gone to market with a fashion buyer. I tell my own children that if there is something that captures their interest, then they need to do the research , make contact with professionals in that field, and arrange a day to go see what the job is all about. Then all I have to be willing to do is provide the transportation.

Do you homeschool them for driver's ed?

I don't. I like my children too much to ever try to teach them to drive. My eldest has horrific hand-eye coordination and I'd like to live long enough to see the baby get to drive someday. Getting into the car with the 15-year-old would not be good for me or for our relationship. The cost of driving school has been worth every single penny. I do know people who have done it successfully and lived to tell the tale, so it can be done.

Check the local laws to be sure that homeschooling driver's ed is legal in your state. Get the materials and study them ahead of time. Then pray. A lot. That's always a good idea, but even more so when your child is getting behind the wheel of a 2,000-pound death machine. (What? Am I the only one who thinks that way?)

Can homeschooled students take AP classes and get credit for them?

Yes, of course they can. The Advanced Placement test is administered by College Board (the SAT people) every year, and are simply tests of a student's knowledge in various curriculum areas. If a student scores high enough on that test, he is awarded college credit for the work that he did in high school. If you have a highly motivated student, I recommend looking in to AP classes and testing. Not only will he start college a few credit hours ahead, but it will look great on his college application. (I'm always trying to build the high school resume.)

As I mentioned earlier in this chapter, dual credit/concurrent enrollment classes at your local community college can be a great opportunity for your student. In many states, public and private school students are allowed to take classes at their local colleges and have the credits they earn count for both high school and college. (You actually *can* get two birds with one stone!) Many states (call your local college and ask) pick up most of the cost of the classes and parents pay for books and student fees. This has meant that our eldest has been able to take college classes for less than $200 a piece including those ridiculously expensive college text books. If she continues at her current rate, she will graduate high school next year one credit hour shy of being a college sophomore. She will have saved herself an entire year. That's an educational incentive that really appeals to her!

Check with your local college, homeschool support groups, co-ops, and message boards to see what kinds of opportunities are available in your area. Like all things homeschool, you may have to drive a bit to get there, but the hassle is definitely worth it.

My mom can't believe that I'd rob my children of the opportunity of going to high school. What do I say to that?

You can thank Hollywood – and grandma's faulty memory – for the fairy tale that high school was an amazing experience and should never be missed. I will admit that there were some really fun parts: football rivalries, marching band, the cute boy in the lunch room, pep rallies, etc. The thing these happy moments all have in common is that they are social and not academic experiences. Nobody ever sits and waxes rhapsodic over Mr. Torres's Chemistry class or Mrs. Pettit's grammar quizzes. Grandparents talk about the fun and the excitement of being young and with their friends. Guess what? Your kids will be young and have friends too. While they may not have the same experiences you or your parents had, they will have experiences which are uniquely their own. While a part of the difference will be due to homeschooling, the bigger part will be because the culture has changed.

The truth is that the majority of teen socialization these days isn't happening in the hallways of the local high school. It's going on via text message, Instagram, and Facebook. Electronic media has completely changed the ways that teenagers connect with each other. When we were this age, we passed paper notes in chemistry class. The kids are still passing notes; they're just using their phones to do it.

Sites such as Facebook have been an invaluable tool in allowing teens to have many of the "normal" kid experiences while being homeschooled. These websites are where the planning happens. It's where one kid will say to his friends, "Who's going to the game on Friday?" or "What are the plans for the weekend? Anyone want to get together and hang out?" The planning and hanging out that we used to do during lunch in the cafeteria, is now done with Facetime, Skype, or group text messaging. Cell phones and the internet have made it possible for homeschooled students to have social lives that are virtually identical to their traditionally schooled peers. Your children will have friends, and they will have adventures to regale their children with some day.

Homeschooled high school students are not, generally speaking, spending their weekend sitting at home reading Voltaire. They are normal teenagers who just happen to go to school at the kitchen table. Their friends come from co-ops, sports teams, church youth group, volunteer organizations, and the local homeschool support group. These are normal kids with friends and social lives. By homeschooling your high school students, you're not robbing them of normal high school experiences. With so many children now being homeschooled, they won't be weird, they'll just be one of the many different varieties of what normal has now come to mean.

Okay, but what about prom?

Prom. Oh my goodness. If I had a dollar for every time I hear someone say "But what about the prom?" I'd have whole lotta dollars. Prom has become some sort of rite of passage to adulthood. There used to be Bar Mitzvahs or Confirmations, now we have the prom.

Don't worry. Your kids can go to prom if they want. Most major cities will have at least one homeschool group hosting their own prom. If there isn't one in your area, then you might look into hosting one or even travelling a bit. Your child can also go as the date of one of his public or privately schooled friends. Silly or not, it's an American tradition, and if your child really wants to participate (as long as you have no objection) there's probably nothing stopping him. Besides, those pictures of your child all dressed up for the prom may be just what the doctor ordered to finally get grandma on your side!

TEN

Co-ops and Support Groups

"Nobody has ever before asked the nuclear family to live all by itself in a box the way we do. With no relatives, no support, we've put it in an impossible situation." – Margaret Mead

What is the difference between a co-op and a support group?

A support group is exactly what it sounds like. It's a group of homeschooling parents who come together either in real life or online to provide one another advice, moral support, an encouraging audience, a fresh perspective, or even just an adult voice. Some meet regularly and offer field trips, parties, and play dates, while others never come together because they are nothing more than on-line message boards. They can consist of a group of friends who already knew each other before they began teaching, or a thousand women who have never met. A support group can have formal rules with elected officers and a set schedule of divided duties, or it can be a loose collective of like–minded mothers of similarly-aged children. When it's the right fit, a support group can provide the sister you want, the good friends you need, and the mother figure you wish you had. The easiest way to find one is to ask around or to Google "homeschool support group (fill in your town here)" to find one near you, or just "homeschool group" if location doesn't matter.

A co-op is a different thing entirely. It's a group of families (perhaps an off-shoot of a support group) dedicated to sharing the responsibility of educating its members' children. You've heard, I'm sure, of a farmer's cooperative, where individual farmers donate their time to each other's crops thereby helping everyone involved? A homeschool co-op is very much the same thing. Parents, usually moms, swap the teaching of classes with one another. For instance, I'm a big math nerd. I love it, but I hate teaching art. The messiness, the prep work, the coming up with ideas...it's overwhelming to me. My friend, Beth, loves the creativity and joy of teaching art, so every Monday we get together and I teach math to everyone, and she teaches art. When our friend Carolyn wanted to join she agreed to teach the science lessons she's so good at organizing. That way, all three of us get a break from the things we struggle with, and the children get the benefit of teachers who are good at their subjects.

As you might imagine, homeschoolers really want help with teaching certain subjects, especially in the upper grades. As a result more formal co-ops have sprung up in many areas. These larger co-ops offer a wide variety of classes, and often have certified teachers. Classes typically take place once or twice a week with moms overseeing homework and possibly doing some or all of the grading. While some co-ops will accept a donation of time in exchange for tuition, many more will require tuition be paid either to the co-op itself or to each individual teacher. It is, in essence, a mini-private school for homeschooled students.

As with most things having to do with homeschooling, the distinction between a support group and a co-op can get blurry. Some co-ops have the fringe benefit of a great parent support system, and many support groups offer limited classes or educational field trips. No matter what they're called, a good one can be a life saver to any homeschooler who needs it.

How do I know if I need a support group and how do I find one?

That will depend entirely on how much support you need. Do you have a supportive family? Do you know veteran homeschooling families who are ready and willing to help you? Do your children have a circle of friends? If you already have these things in place, you are a very lucky woman! You may not need to go in search of a support group. If you're not so fortunate, it's not a bad thing to consider.

If you are in a small town or rural area, you may not find many groups from which to choose. In fact, you may seem to be the only homeschooler around, which can be very lonely. If this is you, I can't stress enough the value of an online message board or Yahoo! group. You're not the only person in the world in your situation, and it helps to be reminded of that and know where to find supportive people. You can start with a good old fashioned Google search, look on Facebook, and from there go to a search of

Yahoo! groups. There are groups for every kind of homeschooling family you can imagine, so try a broad search, but don't be afraid to narrow it down. A search of the terms: Catholic, homeschool, message board, and elementary school will get you to love2learn.blogpsot.com. There you will find the link to the 4 real learning forum (which I love!) Also check out Catholic Homeschool Support (catholichomeschool.org). On their page you'll find a wealth of resources, links, and information. The information is always changing as new things are added, so be sure to check back every few months to see what's new.

If you're in a larger area, I'd still recommend starting your search online. Additionally, I'd ask at the bookstore where you buy supplies to see if they have any contact information for homeschoolers. Call your local churches and ask about a homeschooling group. Your priest or pastor will probably have a pretty good idea of who the homeschooling families are in your church, so ask him to introduce you. While there may not be a group listed in the bulletin, the secretary might know someone to call. Our church secretary sent many new homeschoolers my way once I gave her permission to do so. If you're looking for people, you might let her know that you're willing to be a parish contact. I've even found groups by calling my local Catholic school. (The school secretary knows way more than people give her credit for knowing.) If she doesn't have a number handy, she may just know where to find it for you.

If you've looked and looked and can't find one or can't find one that you like, you may have to start one up yourself. It will be fine, I promise. You can do this. Heck, if you can take the leap of faith to educate your children at home, you can certainly run a Yahoo! group.

What do I look for in a support group?

I would start by looking for a group that sounds like you. Are you a more formal girl who would like a group which describes itself as "The Consecrated St. _____ Catholic Home School Apostolate, unceasingly faithful to the Magisterium in submission to the Pope and the Bishops in communion with him, serves the Catholic home school families of the Archdiocese..." or are you a little more laid back like this group "This is a free-wheeling, plain-speaking group of women. We try to help and support each other in our homeschooling and motherhood experiences – everything from what do you think of this math program, to what color to paint the kitchen. All members are required to bring both their love of God and their senses of humor." These are the descriptions of two groups I've helped run over the years. I was infinitely more comfortable with the second group because it was a better fit. As you can see, these groups have a very different vibe. While both of them do very good things in the homeschool community, they are very different groups. One has rules and bylaws and a set structure, and the other tries to be more like a group of girlfriends. Since the majority of groups don't cost anything to join, I'd try any that seems as if it might fit. You can always quit those that aren't your speed and no hard feelings. Even the groups that weren't a good fit for our family introduced us to people we came to love.

Secondly, I would try to find a group with families who have children the ages of mine. Some groups are geared toward K-5 and others to high school families; still others will have families with a wide variety of ages. If your baby is a junior in high school, you aren't going to find friends for him by hanging out with the kindergarten moms. They can be a lot of fun and support for *you,* but then you'll have to continue searching for his peers.

Third, find out what kind of time commitment the group requires, if any. Do you have that kind of time to give? Scheduling one field trip a year is not a big deal, but volunteering every month can be. How does your calendar look and how easily do you get overwhelmed? It's so easy for novice homeschoolers to over-commit at the beginning of the year. You're full of excitement and enthusiasm and it doesn't seem like once a month is all that much. I would recommend hanging back if possible and seeing how hectic your life is once you have a full schedule of classes and activities.

Fourth, if it's a support group run by a different faith group or denomination, or even a secular group, see what their policies are for membership. There are some amazing groups who are warm and welcoming to people of other faiths or denominations, while there are others that require all members to sign a statement of faith. Make sure to read through the statement of faith carefully as Catholics and those of some other faiths may not be able to sign it. If it's a secular group, what are its rules for discussions of subjects of faith? Do they mind if you mention Christmas or Easter projects? Find out how strict they are and decide whether or not you can live with that.

I'm thinking maybe I need to start my own support group. What's an easy way to get started?

If you already know a few other homeschooling families (it doesn't have to be a lot – two or three is fine to start), and your children are young, then start simple. Consider a field trip club, moms' night out group, or a show and tell group.

In a field trip group, the members agree on how often they want to get together: every other week, once a month, every two months, etc. Either you, or a rotating mom in charge, would be responsible for organizing each trip. Don't panic about the planning. It can be as simple as "next Tuesday, let's all meet at the zoo from 2-4. Bring your own snacks." Most moms just need a date in order to have the motivation to make things happen. It can be as laid back or as detailed as you choose to make it. Organize it through email. Set up a Yahoo! group calendar to keep everyone in the loop. The moms get to talk and hang out while the kids run and play with each other. Easy peasy.

Moms' night out can be great when you have moms with various ages of children. If yours are in kindergarten but the other two moms have children in high school, it can be awkward to plan school activities together. That doesn't mean you shouldn't be friends. You can learn a lot from her experience (even if she's a new homeschooler too, she's kept her children alive longer than you have), so take the kids out of the equation. Pick a regular night to get together and let Dad keep the kids while you network a bit. Meet at a restaurant or trade houses and have everyone bring hors d'oevres and a bottle of wine. It doesn't matter where you are, or even if you discuss homeschooling at all. It's about hanging out with other women like you and enjoying their company. Whether there are two of you or 20, the important part is to relax and have a good time.

Show-and-Tell is my absolute favorite kind of support group/mini co-op blend. I love it! It's the perfect opportunity for your children to show off the poetry they've memorized, the dioramas they've built, or the soccer participation trophy they got last weekend. Even more than that, it's one of those invaluable socialization exercises disguised as getting together with friends. It takes two or more families, and a house where you can meet. The children take turns getting up in front of the group (learning public speaking skills) while the others listen and pay attention (listening skills). In our group, the speaker begins by introducing himself (no matter how well the audience already knows him) and gives his age. He then tells about whatever he has brought or prepared for the day. He has to stand still – no fidgeting (as much as possible) – and speak slowly and clearly. We expect his audience to sit still, be quiet, and pay attention. We let the speaker take questions at the end, and we've yet to have one who doesn't get at least a few. The audience has to raise hands and wait to be called on, which teaches them patience and respect. Afterwards, we have lunch and the moms get to visit while the kids run and play. My children and those in our show-and-tell group beg for it; there are tears when we tell them "it's not today." It is super easy to organize, doesn't need the children to be exactly the same ages or grade levels (in fact it's a good thing to have some variety), and all it requires from you is an email reminder and a clean-ish house.

How about a co-op? How do I find one of those?

You will find a co-op much the same way as a support group, through internet searches and word of mouth. Any family near you who has been homeschooling for more than a few years will know where to find them if they exist in your area. They will also know which ones are good and which not so much (if you are lucky enough to have more than one from which to choose.)

What should I look for in a co-op?

If it is a small co-op run by friends or acquaintances, find out what classes they are going to offer, who will be doing the teaching, and what they want you to teach. Then ask yourself if you can teach that. What will happen if someone's child loses interest or drops out? Will his mom continue teaching the class anyway, or will you be scrambling to figure it out midyear? Who is responsible for grading, the mom or the mom teaching the class? Who is going to be in the class, and will there be anyone holding the others back? What is the policy for behavioral issues? Can a student be asked to leave one class but still remain in the others? Where will it take place? If it's a private house, is there a back-up in case of sickness or if the host family elects to leave the group?

If it is the private school model of co-op, the beginning questions of age, grade level, and classes offered are the same. Additionally, you will need to find out the membership requirements for each family. Ask about the time commitment for your family. Are member families asked to volunteer or is it a requirement? How much is the tuition and is it figured per student or per class? Is there a multi-child discount available? Is the co-op accredited and/or are the classes recognized and accepted by the local school districts? Who are the teachers and what are their qualifications? What facilities are available? Is there space for science experiments to take place? Is there time for socializing? Is the socializing supervised and by whom? Do they offer graduation ceremonies for seniors? What types of students attend the co-op and are they people with whom our family would get along? Is there a religious component to any of the classes and can your student opt out of any part you find objectionable?

An athletic co-op is generally for junior high and/or high school students and offers sports and athletics such as football, basketball, or cheerleading which would normally only be available in a traditional school setting. Competing against small public and private schools, they give students an opportunity for experiences they would otherwise miss out on while homeschooling. Find out whether there is a Statement of Faith requirement. If you can't sign it, you can't play. What will the co-op cost? What kind of equipment will you be asked to provide? Who will be coaching and what kind of experience do they have? Will there be support staff and athletic trainers available in case of injury? Will the team be providing transportation to out-of-town games, or will each family be responsible for its own player? Is there fundraising required and how much of it do you have to do? Most importantly, does your student want to play?

It all sounds really good. Is there a downside to it?

There can be. It would be dishonest of me to write this chapter and not mention the drama that can be all too common in homeschooling circles. In 11 years, I've seen many groups come and go. In that time I've learned that there is nothing more destructive than a bored stay-at-home mom who's looking for drama. There is no limit to the lengths some women will go. I had no idea. Truly.

There is girl drama everywhere and in all walks of life. It's all about picking the people you associate with carefully. If you have good instincts, then trust them. If you have a checkered history in the judgment department, then hold back and watch for a bit. You'll figure out who the pot stirrers are quickly enough.

Support groups and co-ops can definitely be worth the work and the effort involved in finding them, and I wouldn't let a few rotten apples ruin it for me if I were you. There can be drama in any group, and while it's never any fun, it shouldn't deter you from joining up with the other homeschoolers in your area. In both the local and online groups you will find amazing women who can mentor you through the early days and offer you their hard-won wisdom. The friendships and camaraderie in these groups can be invaluable boosts to help get you through the rough times and celebrate your victories. No one will ever quite get the joy of hearing your child read his very first book the way these moms will.

ELEVEN

Socialization

I'm sure the reason such young nitwits are produced in our schools is because they have no contact with anything of use in everyday life.
– Petronius (a.d. 66)

I keep hearing "What about socialization?" from everyone. What's the deal?

Socialization is the big boogey man of homeschooling to those who haven't ever actually taught their children at home. It's a question that strikes right at the core of what we are doing, because what good will an amazing education do your children if they don't have the social skills necessary to be part of society?

I don't know where the idea began that the only place children can learn social skills is inside a traditional school. It's just not true. Socialization – the process by which people learn societal norms and how to behave in public – doesn't happen in any one place. It happens in every place. Unless you plan on locking your children in the basement and never letting them out in public, they're going to learn how to be around other people.

Your children will play with the neighborhood children, meet people in Sunday school, volunteer in their community, participate in co-ops, and take dance classes.

They will be in Scouts, Little League, book clubs, and spelling bees. Your kids will discover online forums, field trips, park days, and theater classes. Far from being isolated from other people, they will have a seemingly endless array of social opportunities where they can meet other people, make friends, and work on their social skills.

When it comes to socialization, homeschooled children actually have a leg up on their traditionally schooled peers. While school kids are spending 8 hours a day segregated into classrooms by age and grade level, homeschooled children are encountering people of all ages and social groups. Homeschooled students learn from an early age how to relate to people of different ages, abilities, and ethnicities out in the real world. Their friends will not be determined by who's sitting next to them in their classroom, but by the kinds of people they enjoy hanging out with.

While at first glance it may seem that kids in a regular classroom will enjoy a social life that homeschooled students can't, that just isn't the way it works out in practice. Far from being sheltered and awkward, most homeschooled students have lives that are just as friend-filled, busy, and normal as you could wish for them to be.

Well, I just don't want my children to be freaks.

You don't? Why not? From what I can see, a freak is simply someone who is outside other people's definition of normal, which makes me a freak. Seven children and homeschooling? That's almost the textbook definition of freak. If you are going to homeschool your children, then you need to know that they're going to be a little bit freaky too. How could they help it when they've got a pair of big ol' homeschooling freaks for parents?

So, I have to ask: why are you letting other people define what normal is for your child? Why are you letting people *you don't trust to educate them* dictate what limits they should live within? I say "Let them color outside the lines. Let them be the weird and wonderful people God has planned for them to be!"

Freaks are the people who change the world and keep it interesting. They're the nerd who started a computer company in his garage, the one who won the spelling bee, the girl who used her microwave to create plasma (the state of matter, not the blood product), the priest who sets hearts on fire, or the artist who is touted as the next Picasso. These are the nerdy freaks of this world. They are the ones who create, think, and dream. They are the kind of people we all hope to raise.

Think back to high school. What made the "cool kids" cool was that they had an air of boredom. Do you want to raise bored and boring people, or do you want to raise people who are excited by life? Raise freaks and be proud that you do.

So, you're saying that I shouldn't worry about the freak thing?

That's exactly what I'm saying. Freaks are cool. What you should be worried about is their being socially awkward. Socially awkward is to be avoided like it's the plague. It can't actually kill you, but it can sure feel that way.

How do we avoid the socially awkward then?

The only way to learn how to behave with other people is to practice it. While social skills come more easily to some people than to others, they are a skill which anyone can learn.[1] Yes, some people are naturally gifted at this and others are not. That's to be expected. It's like throwing a baseball. Some people are great at it and become professional ball players, and some only barely manage to get the ball to go in front of them. The more practice you get though, the better your aim and the further it goes.

Your children need regular exposure to other children. They do not need to be exclusively around kids their own age, and I would even caution you against that. There's something a little unnatural about the tendency of school children to hang out only with people their own age. When they grow up they won't go find the 23-year-old company where all the 23-year- olds are and work there until age 24.

---

[1] If your child is living on the autism spectrum or has a social disorder, that's another matter. Professional guidance will be your best resource for helping your child.

They'll go out and get a job in an office with people of all ages with whom they will have to work. If they haven't learned to relate to people younger and older than them in their childhoods, when should they learn it?

Learning social skills and how to relate to other people should be just a regular part of your child's life. For example, here's a rundown of my 13-year-old son's day:

- Woke up early, took a shower, and got dressed.
- Helped his 3-year-old brother get changed out of his pajamas and dressed for the day.
- Argued with his sister over the last of the cereal before deciding to make eggs.
- The little kids saw that eggs were being made; he ended up making breakfast and the two little boys as well as himself.
- Discussed his pre-Algebra with me because he just didn't get what the book was saying.
- During lunch, he texted his best friend and made plans to meet up in the afternoon.
- Walked the neighbors' dogs as part of his pet-sitting business, then texted his customers to tell them that their dogs were happy.
- For his history project, he called his 92-year-old great grandmother to ask her about living through the Dust Bowl and Great Depression.
- Rode his bike to the library to pick up the books they were holding for him. It took a while because he always stops to chat with the librarian.

- Stopped at a potential pet-sitting customer's house on the way home to meet the dog and its owner. He decided that the owner wasn't that nice and that he didn't want to work for him.
- Went to his best friend's house to write the script for the movie they are making.
- Over dinner, got into a heated debate with his 11-year-old brother about which was a better film adaptation - *Harry Potter* or *The Hunger Games*.
- Went to youth group where he spent 45 minutes in class and 45 minutes hanging out with the guys.
- Led family bedtime prayers. (It was his turn.)

Social skills are picked up everywhere your children go. They're going to run into people of all ages. They will meet people who like them and people who don't. There will be those who want to chat and be friendly and others who are strictly professional. That's okay. That's the way life works. No two people are alike, and they're not always going to be nice. It happens. It's all a great opportunity for your children to learn how to be polite and get along with even the not-so-nice ones – that's what socialization is all about.

So, I know about some of the obvious routes to socialization: kids can join a sports team through a local youth club or learn to share by doing so with

siblings. What are some of the less obvious social skills they need?

Being responsible for themselves is absolutely one of the most overlooked life skills. One of the benefits that traditionally schooled students have over ours is that they learn to speak up for themselves. A child in school learns to interact with teachers, the school librarian, coaches, teacher aides, etc. They learn to articulate clearly their wants and needs to adults who are not members of their family. If he wants to play a sport, he puts his own name on the sign-up sheet. If his homework isn't turned in on time, he's got to face the music by himself. If he doesn't want the gross green beans for lunch, he has to be able to say so.

I have to admit that my natural bent is to over-help my children. At the library, I tended ask for the books they needed. If they wanted to play sports, I would be the one to register them. It's something I've had to force myself to stop doing, because my intervention hamstrings them. It was the day a coach told me to back off – because mine was the only daughter who needed her mommy in order to have a conversation – that I stopped.

This can all seem so simple that you may forget all about it. When you pump gas, bring cash and send your child into the station to pay before you pump. When you go out to eat, let them decide what they want (within reason) and order for themselves. Being clear and polite can be very hard for some children. When the sport seasons begin, hand your children the phone and let them put their own names on the list. Force them to step out of the "mommy bubble" and begin to do things in their own world that public school kids do in theirs.

You'll learn how to build these lessons into all of your outings. If you are in public then your children have to know how to behave like human beings. Why would you waste the opportunity? Not every lesson has to be big. Being sure to thank the girl who checks you out at the grocery store is an important thing for someone who's 2 to learn. It's even more important when your son is 15 and seems to have lost the ability to speak in anything other than a grunt. Manners matter in this world, and being friendly counts. Practice both at every opportunity.

You will find that your children will gain confidence as they step out in the world and learn to talk to adults with respect and authority. Your children need to learn both the life skills necessary to interact in the adult world and the ability to move easily within it.

If I have an only child, will I have to work harder at this?

Yes, you will. Children with siblings have the advantage of being forced to practice getting along with others every day of their lives. Children with a lot of siblings will get to practice it even more often. There is something wonderful about other people in your household that teaches compromise, patience, and tolerance faster than anything else does. If your child doesn't have that built in, then you have to seek out opportunities for him to learn it. Invite other children over to your house, so that he can get used to having other people on his turf. Make sure that he has a chance to be forced to compromise. Hang out with groups of other children (friends with big families are a great resource for you) so that he can learn to function within a group dynamic.

On the upside, only children have the gift of their parents' whole attention. If God has given you one child, you have opportunities to get out and about that larger families find more difficult logistically. You can tailor your outings and activities to your child's interests. Because you don't have to plan your activities around naps and whining siblings, there's nothing to stop your forays out into the world except your own imaginations. You could take your ballet lover to see every local production of *The Nutcracker*. I happen to know from experience that it's easier to get one single ballet fan backstage to meet the principle dancers than it is to get a whole group back there. You can take your horse lover to the race track to meet the jockeys and trainers. They are often willing to take just a child or two through race day preps. Where a larger group would spook the horses, one is a welcome visitor. The key is to get out into the world to meet as many people as possible. Since you don't have a wide variety of personalities at your kitchen table, you get to go in search of them. Just imagine the adventures the two of you will have!

Most of the people in our area are very much the same. Where do I go for a little diversity?

There are few things as exciting as introducing children to new people and new cultures. The music, food, clothing, and customs add a delightful variety to the make-up of our world. A very simple way to introduce different cultures, if you live in an area which is not very diverse, is to seek out restaurants, shops, and supermarkets that cater to different groups of people. Check the internet or phone book for listings. You can buy spices at the Indian grocery, eat dinner at the Thai restaurant, shop in the Asian market, or pick up a little something at the Mexican import shop. Make sure that you and your children stop and chat with the people everywhere you go. Ask them where they've come from and what brought them here. Have the waitress in the restaurant recommend her favorite food from the menu, and try it! If there are dancers and musicians, then get up and dance!

Exposing ourselves and our children to different cultures and customs is one of the easiest and most fun ways to learn about people and the world. The more time you spend outside your comfort zone, the more your children will learn that people are pretty much the same all over the world. It's an important lesson, and one that homeschoolers really have the time to enjoy learning.

So it's really possible to turn out socially acceptable human beings without putting them in school?

Not only is it possible; you've got a better than average chance! Homeschooling produces some of the nicest people you can ever hope to meet. I think the difference lies in their role models. While traditionally schooled kids are looking up to and emulating their peers (those darn "cool kids"), homeschooled students' role models tend to be the adults around them. Children whose primary role models are adults will be more mature and better prepared for adult society.

Rather than spending their childhoods in a school-enforced peer-group, homeschooled children grow up in a world where friendships aren't determined by age, grade-level, and seating charts. Because they haven't been raised in the school system, homeschooled students bypass the disdain for adults and dependence on peer approval that seems to define modern American kids. That means that they tend to be happier kids who are more comfortable with who they are.

TWELVE

The Mistakes We All Make...

Read This and Maybe You Won't Have To

"Isn't it nice to think that tomorrow is a new day with no mistakes in it yet?" – L.M. Montgomery

What mistakes do you see new homeschoolers making?

These are the most common mistakes homeschooling moms make, no matter how long they've been doing this:

Trying to recreate public school at your kitchen table

You have chosen to homeschool your children for a reason. What was that reason? If it had something to do with how traditional schooling wasn't in the best interest of your child, why would you try to recreate what you've already admitted won't work? If doing so sounds like setting yourself up for failure, you're right!

Traditional school classrooms are the way they are because having a standard method of operation makes the school run better. It's about conformity and crowd control. Those aren't issues you are dealing with, so you have the opportunity to ditch them. Here are just a few of the places you don't have to follow the rules:

- It's okay for your children to call you Mom during the school day and not "Mrs."

- You don't need to stand in front of your student and lecture her; you can sit on the couch and talk the lesson over together.

- You don't need report cards – they're designed to let parents know how their kids are doing in school.

- Recess doesn't have to happen at a certain time of the day, but can take place whenever wiggling starts to interfere with the lessons.

- Vacations can happen when it's convenient for your family, not just during the summer break.

- You don't have to take a summer vacation.

- Your day doesn't have to start at 8:00 or end at 3:00. Let your early risers start at 6:30, if that works for you, and your late sleepers get started closer to noon.

Strict schedules and written-in-stone deadlines don't always work when you're teaching at home. They don't take into account the history lesson that takes days longer than you'd originally planned, the week mom spent in bed with the flu, or the days Grandpa came and took everyone fishing. One of the great benefits of homeschooling your children is the flexibility it allows for life to happen. If you are too stuck on what it's supposed to look like, especially if that picture is from a traditional school, you're going to have days (weeks? years?) of frustration.

Trying to make your homeschool look like someone else's

Many new homeschooling moms are scared of doing the wrong thing. They may also be eager to "fit in" with the homeschoolers they know, both online and in real life. This leads to one of the most common rookie mistakes: forgetting who you and your family really are.

Is your family spontaneous or do you thrive within the framework of a schedule? Do you like desks or do your children like to curl up on the sofa? Do you like to tell stories to get your point across or do you just state it straight out there? No two families will come up with the same answers, and that's okay. Your family is unique and wonderful and the way you do things works for you in the rest of your life. Why would you try to change what's working into a reflection of someone else's family? It doesn't make any sense, does it?

Yes, you should ask other families what books they've chosen. Find out from them what teaching methods work with their children. Investigate everything you can, and be sure to ask the reasons why they do (or do not) enjoy what they're doing. Gathering information is always a good thing to do. You will always be able to learn at least a little bit from the experiences of other families. Once you have the information you need, take an honest look at your own family and see how the answers you got from others would fit in with the children you actually have.

It may take a lot of trial and error before you find the best approach for you and your children, but you will get there. You don't need to copy anybody else.

Unrealistic expectations

Parents of young children try to push them too far too fast. This leads to rebellion in the child who is frustrated with not being able to accomplish what mom wants. It wears mom out as she tries every trick she can think of to get her child to perform. This isn't a trick pony; it's your child!

You have to take the time to educate yourself about what is developmentally normal. The University of Michigan provides an excellent reference website on this topic that I have bookmarked, stuck on Pinterest, and even written down in my lesson plan book. It is www.med.umich.edu/yourchild/topics/devmile.htm. Buy or check out from the library a book on child development. Even if you ultimately decide not to homeschool, educate yourself in this area. It will save you and your child a whole lot of heartache and unnecessary frustration.

I spoke on the phone yesterday to a mother whose daughter could not hold her pencil correctly. No matter how many times she was corrected or what kinds of pencils or grips they tried, the little girl just couldn't do it. "How can I hope to teach her anything if I can't even teach her how to hold a pencil?" the mother asked me. Her daughter is 2 ½. She doesn't have the motor skills or muscle control to be able to hold the pencil even if she could understand what her mom wanted, which she can't....because she's 2. I told her mother to spend time just playing with her daughter and working on pre-writing skills. Teach her to sing the ABC's. Have her string beads or cereal to build up her fine motor skills so that when she's ready to write, she can! Let her color any old which way she wants, because she's only going to be little for a short time. At her age learning should look like play, because that's what is developmentally appropriate.

With older children, I see the opposite. Moms often will not expect as much from their children as they are capable of doing. Teenagers are difficult. The conventional wisdom tells parents to "pick our battles," so we let due dates slide and look the other way when what's turned in is shoddy. Mom lets her baby read the abridged version instead of the real book because "it's too hard." Mothers look at a challenging curriculum and judge it to be "too much." Really? For the 15-year-old who taught herself to play the guitar and can sing the entire score of *Les Miserables* from memory?

Masked as being "realistic," these under-expectations may really be an excuse to avoid challenging a truculent teen. But we do them a disservice when we fail to expect from our teens what they have the potential to accomplish. A mediocre curriculum will leave your children bored (and bored children get into trouble). Mom will be left wondering why it isn't working and end up disappointed in herself.

I'm here to tell you that with school, you have to pick *all* the battles. There isn't any single one of them where you can let it slide. Due dates are an important life skill. His someday-boss isn't going to care that the work was hard; he's just going to want it done. Mama's baby had better be able to do the work or figure out how to get it done or he's going to be fired. Moms need to learn how to help their children without making it so easy or lax that they get in the way of the teen's growth to adulthood.

Over or under-scheduling

You can't do it all unless you have unlimited financial resources and unlimited time. It really just isn't possible. If you've figured out the whole saintly bilocation deal, can you share with the rest of us? I'd love to be literally in two places at one time. You're only human, girl, you need to relax and learn to let it go a little bit.

Over-scheduling is a trap that ensnares too many novice and veteran homeschoolers. There are a dizzying number of field trips, group activities, and classes available to your students; that doesn't mean that you have to do them all. You don't even have to *try* to do them all. You will have years and years to see and do all of the things you want your children to experience. (No one says it all has to be done in the first year.) Set a regular time in your schedule for outings, pick a set day for outside classes, and (I can't stress the importance of this enough) stick with your game plan. Trying to do too much will make you crazy. I've lost count of the moms who spent whole days in the car with their children. The kids attempt to do schoolwork in the backseat while their siblings are in band or art class. Is it possible to have good penmanship in the back of the car? Could you learn math there or remember your history facts? Your children can't either. Don't set them up to fail.

Don't go the opposite route either and chronically under-schedule. Having a set time for schoolwork is a wonderful thing. Never leaving the house in the name of slogging through the curriculum can stunt your children's development. They need to see the light of day. So many wonderful activities exist for your family to see and experience. Why wouldn't you take your kids to see and do them? If you are fortunate enough that your local museum has mummies, you should go and visit them during the month you're studying Ancient Egypt. Get out of the house and see what's out there. Even the trip itself can be a geography and map-reading lesson. It isn't healthy for your children always to be stuck at home, and it will make you a wild-eyed lunatic. You don't want to be that girl. Plan a field trip or two.

In our house, all field trips happen on Fridays and extra classes happen on Tuesday or Thursday afternoons. I've intentionally written the lesson plans with this schedule in mind. On the weeks we don't have a place to go, we enjoy a quiet afternoon together at home just playing. While I've learned the importance of scheduling (which has never been my strong suit), I've also learned that being flexible and spontaneous are vital too. We missed the King Tut exhibit when it toured the United States because I refused to change my plans, by golly. Who knows if my kids will get the opportunity to see it again outside of Cairo? A little more flexibility on my part would have meant an *amazing* educational opportunity for them. But I stuck firmly to my schedule, so it didn't happen. I've learned for next time to drop everything and go if the opportunity warrants it.

Spending way too much

You can't buy a good education. You just can't. Spending too much is a serious temptation for every homeschooling mom. Buying every book in the catalog, purchasing the most expensive curriculum, and signing up for every available class will not guarantee the academic success of your children. What it can do is stress your family finances to the point where you have to consider taking a job just to pay the violin teacher. Don't do this to your family!

Here's how we keep from going broke while homeschooling seven children:

- Sit down with your husband and review your finances before you begin purchasing books or signing up for anything. Knowing what you have to work with before you begin will help keep you from going wildly over budget.

- Make a wish list of books for every child. Actually write them down along with what they cost. It's amazing to me just how many books I eliminate from my list once I actually see the subtotal. I edit and rearrange in order to get most of what I want for what I want to spend. Great materials aren't a blessing if they land us in the poorhouse. (I have to remind myself of that often.)

- Don't go to the curriculum fair or homeschool convention without your wish list, and then stick to it! My personal rule is that if I find something I like better, I have to take one thing off of my list. Those book fairs are like crack for homeschooling moms. I swear to you that I've spent more money on goofy gadgets or the latest handwriting program I'd never heard of before that moment because they just looked so cool on the shelf. It's so easy to get caught up in it all. For the most sorely tempted I'd even recommend bringing along a frugal friend. When her eyes get wide at the pile of stuff you're carrying, maybe you'll stop.

- Search online for used copies of the most expensive books. You can save some serious money. For example, my eldest daughter's Geometry book was listed new at $119, but I found a used copy on exlibris.com for $.98. We purchased Rosetta Stone Spanish from Craig's list for half its retail price. You can find what you need, but you have to be patient and have the money put aside so that you can jump on a deal when you find it.

- Sign up for the educator discounts anywhere that allows you to do so. The discounts I have found average around 15%. At Barnes and Noble, for example, the discount is 20% and can be used on anything in the store (including toys and games!!) except music or magazines. This rocks come Christmas time!

- Buy non-consumable books whenever possible if you have more than one child. This will save you tons of money down the road.

- If only there were a place in your hometown where you could borrow books for free...Oh wait! There is! It's called the library. Sitting right there on the shelves in the library will be most of the books you will need for your literature curriculum and for research projects. Many libraries even have textbooks either on hand or available through an inter-library loan program. Get to know the librarian in the children's section. Introduce yourself to her and let her know that you'll be homeschooling this year. Ask her for suggestions and *listen* to her! Our librarian has helped me to develop reading lists that dovetail with whatever we are studying in science or history. This has led to an impressive study of the Great Depression, my son's fanatical interest in steam engines, and my daughter's encyclopedic knowledge of insects...ALL FOR FREE!

- Have you considered trading for the classes you'd like your children to take? If you can teach piano, tutor math, speak a foreign language, or even babysit someone else's children, you may be able to barter for the lessons you'd like your children to have. My sweet, saintly friend does art projects and science experiments with my children (which I not-so-secretly dread doing). I host show-and-tell get-togethers every other Friday because my house is big enough to hold a large group, and I like crowds. It's absolutely a win-win!

- Find the homeschool groups in your area. Many of them are nothing more than a yahoo internet email group and require no time commitment from you. Some are groups with actual get-togethers, meetings, and field trips! Can you say "group discount?" Me, too. There is always some smarty-pants in the area who knows every good deal, free admission day, and secret insider group discount and will post it online for those of us who aren't in the know. I don't know what drives these on-the-ball, super with-it moms, but I'm always delighted to read the new things they've discovered for my family to do.

- Send off for freebies if you see them online. We've scored a working model of the knee from a drug company, story books, free coloring pages to print, and more craft supplies than my children will ever be able to use. I have learned to ask people for things and let them know I'll take what they don't want (within reason). That's how I managed to get an entire set of SRA readers for free. My local public school was throwing them out and I was willing to come and get them.

Failing to invest where it counts

While I'm the self-proclaimed Queen of Cheap, there are some places where it makes sense to spend a little more money.

- I firmly believe in the importance of getting the very best lessons you can. If you have decided that music, dance, art, language, etc. lessons are worth the time and money for your children, it only makes sense to find the very best ones you can afford. If it means driving a bit further, staying a little longer, or cutting out the ice cream on Saturday nights, you will not regret investing in the best instructors available.

- The right curriculum is worth its weight in gold. If you find something that makes your life easier and your children eager to learn, then find a way to afford it if it's at all possible. Budget it in or hold a garage sale, but if it works for your child and you don't have to yell to get him to work, then it is worth every penny you'll spend.

- Buy a copier/printer. Invest in a good one and make sure to check the price of the ink refills before you buy. You're going to be making tons of copies over the years. A good copier will save your textbooks and save you money in the long run. Put this on your list of necessary items and save your pennies until you can buy one. You won't regret the purchase.

Not listening to what your kids are telling you

Mother doesn't always know best, and when you don't, your kids will tell you. You should listen to them. No child should hate math. Ever. I don't know where the idea came from that it was okay for children to cry at the thought of multiplication tables, but it just isn't necessary. They may not like it, but crying should never be a part of it.

If your child squeals with delight when he sees his handwriting book, or eagerly clasps the pencil because it's time for math (even if he's less than enthusiastic, as long as you don't have to fight him every single day)... Congratulations! You've found the right curriculum for your child. It's working. School doesn't have to be miserable. I promise you it doesn't. While it won't always be your children's favorite thing to do, an eager student who is willing to learn means that you're definitely on the right track!

If she curls up in the fetal position at the mention of Phonics, or trembles with dread when science appears, you need to listen up! That curriculum isn't working and you should get rid of it ASAP! I don't care what you paid for it or how thoroughly researched your purchase was, if she hates it, it's the wrong one. Find a curriculum swap and trade that puppy away! Take some pictures and list it on eBay! It doesn't matter what you do, but get rid of it. There's nothing which will sour your student's attitude faster than the torture of books that he hates.

Children naturally love to learn. It's schooling they hate. Have you heard the old saying "find a job you love and you'll never work a day in your life?" It's the same thing with teaching your children. If you find something that touches his mind, you won't have to work so hard to get him to do it. Your children will be honest with you about how it's going. Don't mistake the wrong curriculum for disobedience. If everyone is miserable, change it.

On the other hand, sometimes the tears and complaining have nothing to do with your curriculum choices. It could be the way you're schooling that's not working for your student. If you have set up your day to start early and be finished in time to catch your breath before you start making dinner, that might work for you but not for your teenager who needs to sleep later. By allowing him a few more hours of sleep, you could improve his attitude and ability to learn. We're all cranky and unpleasant when we're tired, and your children are no exception to that rule. Fatigue makes it hard to concentrate and difficult to remember things. If your son is constantly yawning and fighting to stay awake, a delayed start time might bring a huge improvement.

The struggle you're dealing with might also be related to the pace you are setting. Are you going too fast or too slow for your student? If you're moving at a pace that's faster than she can handle, you're inviting frustration that doesn't need to be there. Slow down a bit and don't move forward until you're sure she's got it. It might not be that the math is too hard, but that you're pushing her along faster than she can go. If you give her a chance to digest all the information she's getting, she might surprise you with all that she knows. If you're going too slow for your daughter she's going to get bored and disinterested in the material. Watch her when she works. Is she disappointed to be discussing the shapes of molecules *again*? Is she begging to be allowed to move on? Nothing's going to kill her spark of curiosity faster than boredom. You don't have to do everything by the book. If she gets it, move on.

Still other children don't learn well in certain environments. Does your son read better when curled up on the couch than sitting on a hard chair at a desk or table? Does he like to be seated near a window or is that a distraction? Does he like the room a little on the chilly side, or does a cold room make it harder for him to pay attention? Children are affected by their environment, and this can be especially true for some of them. Figuring out where your kids are the most comfortable learning will make their school time less of a battle for all of you.

While it would be nice to have students who are capable of saying "I don't like this math book," "you're going too fast," or "I'd work better on the couch than at the kitchen table," the reality is that most kids don't know what's wrong – they just know it isn't right. You have to pay attention to the clues they are giving you, ask questions more in depth than "What's wrong?" and be willing to constantly tweak what you're doing until you get it right.

Giving the government too much information

I'm fortunate to live in Texas, which is an extremely low regulation state, so this is not one with which I have personal experience. Homeschooling moms in other states, however, report that telling the local authorities too much can be an invitation to scrutiny by the authorities. I can only imagine.

So, here's the skinny:

- Some states require nothing from parents at all (Alaska, Connecticut, Idaho, Illinois, Indiana, Michigan, Missouri, New Jersey, Oklahoma, and Texas), some require only a letter of the intent to homeschool be sent to the local authorities (Alabama, Arizona, California, Delaware, Kansas, Kentucky, Mississippi, Montana, Nebraska, New Mexico, Nevada, Utah, Wisconsin, Wyoming), if your state isn't listed here, it requires a bit more of you. Check on the HSLDA website (www.hslda.org/laws/) for more information on your individual state. (Of course, these things are subject to change. Double check your state's current requirements just to be certain.)

- Fill out whatever forms and provide whatever information is legally required of you. You don't have to add a bunch of stuff to it to justify what you are doing or the choices you have made. Just the facts, ma'am!

- I know that offering everything they ask and more to the school district feels like being super helpful and cooperative, and who doesn't want to be that? The reality is that the information you are providing is none of their business, plain and simple. By providing extras, you *make* those extra tidbits the government's concern and invite it to become involved in your homeschool. Knowledge is power – the more information you offer the district about your schooling, the more power you are handing to them. Keep it simple and only offer what is strictly required by law.

- Be prepared to defend yourself if you have to. States with a lot of regulations have those regulations in place because someone somewhere is not thrilled with what homeschoolers are doing. Know the laws and follow them to the letter. Keep in mind that part of being the girl-in-charge is being ready to defend your family against anything that may be coming your way. It may never come – for most people it never does – but it's not a bad thing to be ready for it just in case. If having to deal with all the red tape ever gets to the point where you'd like to chuck it all... Texas is a great place to raise a family.

Forgetting to pray

In the busy hustle of educating children and running a household, how easy it is to allow your spiritual life to fall away. I have found that when I forget to talk to my Father the rest of my life becomes chaos. Take the time to say the rosary or other prayer, even if it takes all day stopping and starting to do it. Add the Angelus into your regular daily routine. Take a moment to re-center yourself and ask God for strength, wisdom, and patience *before* you reach out to strangle the 8-year-old. It might just keep you from doing it!

The peace and calm of a mom who prays regularly is a gift you can give your children. Prayer forces you to refocus your attention on something outside of yourself and beyond your children. Laser-beam focus doesn't benefit your family members, it burns them. Take the time to turn your mind and heart to Heaven, and then teach your children to do the same. Your whole household will profit from it, and isn't a relationship with God one of the biggest things you're hoping for them to learn? It has to begin somewhere, and prayer is a great place to begin.

THIRTEEN

Special Learning Issues

"If you aren't in over your head, how do you know how tall you are?"
–T.S. Eliot

We all think our kids are amazingly brilliant and head and shoulders above their peers. How do you know if your child is truly gifted and not just the apple of your eye?

Academically gifted children, over and above those who are just smart or good students, are easy to spot in a crowd. They are the great talents, the high achievers. These are the kids that have you running a mental race just to keep pace with them. This kind of giftedness tends to run in families, so if you were a gifted child, your husband was gifted, then there's a good chance that your child may be gifted too.

If it's important to you to "know for sure," you can have your suspected genius tested. A pediatric or developmental psychologist can do a series of tests, including an IQ test, to tell you whether or not your child is above average in intelligence, talent, or understanding. While I can see the value of this label within an institutional school setting, the need for this in a homeschool setting is unclear. Unless you are completely overwhelmed by the pace he's setting and are looking for some outside help, a formal diagnosis has little benefit for a homeschooled gifted child.

If your child is faster or brighter than his or her peers, you're going to know it pretty quickly by watching him with other kids his age. You can also compare notes with other homeschooling moms, and perhaps an educational psychologist. (Take what other moms tell you with a grain of salt. I've learned that moms will often fudge the truth to make themselves feel better or their kids look good. Talk to the honest moms you know. If you're unsure, find a veteran homeschooler with years of experience under her belt.)

Get a diagnosis if you need it for you. Read the myriad of books that have been written on the subject. Otherwise, let it go and just focus on teaching your kid.

Do you do anything different with gifted kids? Do you go wider? Deeper? Both?

YES! We study anything and everything they are interested in knowing. I begin adding in lots of side projects, of a scope and a depth which would overwhelm most other students, and allow for deeper study as a way of throwing the brakes on them a little bit. Who wants to have a child in college at 10? Not me. I've never been convinced that that level of acceleration is in anyone's best interest, though I know there are some who would disagree with that. I also know that sticking strictly to the material and not allowing for exploration is the fastest way to lose the interest of a gifted child.

Academically gifted children crave knowledge and thrive on a challenge. If there isn't one in the curriculum, she will create one. I'd much rather have the challenge be an in-depth study of bread mold, a giant research project on the moon, or a new musical composition than how many times can she kick her brother before I kill her. Bored children become behavioral problems. We all know this is true. If they are bored enough long enough, they'll create their own excitement. I've rarely found that kind of undirected energy to end well, have you?

You're going to have to channel and direct her interest and ability, even if it's something that doesn't interest you in the least. My more advanced children become obsessed with knowing things and we have spent weeks watching YouTube videos of open heart surgery to see how a heart actually beats, or an afternoon dissecting a chicken (you can get one all in one piece from the Asian market, did you know that?) in order to find out what part makes the eggs. These are the moments I live for as an educator. They are the times when curiosity and learning come together in lessons they will never forget.

While children who are academically gifted have been known to race ahead in their school work, it is important to bear in mind that *they are the age that they are.* While it may be appropriate for an advanced 7-year-old to be doing fifth grade work, it's not socially appropriate for him to hang out with fifth graders. Academically he may be at that age, but socially he's a second grader. He needs your help to find friends and playmates among people in his age-group and not his grade-level.

How do you know if it's just a "little bit? How do you know if your kid is a little bit in front of or behind the curve?

We get used to seeing our children every day. We get comfortable with their abilities, whatever speed they are. That's what makes it hard to tell if your child is one side or the other of "average." That's totally okay. In homeschooling, being a little bit off the norm doesn't make much of a difference.

One of the loveliest things about educating your children at home is that you can teach them at whatever pace they need. If he completely "gets it" and wants to fly through the material, there's nothing but your own sanity to stop him from doing a month's worth of work in two days. My eldest daughter rocketed through all of second grade in four months and didn't slow her stride until halfway through third. I got out of her way and let her sprint through the material which was no challenge at all. It really was one of the best decisions I ever made as an educator. When she hit the wall of Geometry in the tenth grade, she had all the time in the world to slow down and really figure it all out. She's definitely on the "little bit" faster side of things, but we've never had her tested. There really never was a need to do so. We just let her run at her own pace and hoped and prayed that I'd be able to keep up with her.

My second daughter has struggled on the other side of things. She's worked harder and longer, with greater determination than most will ever need, in order to learn to read. I don't know if she's actually slower than average, or just the one normal child in a household that is decidedly not. It doesn't matter to us. I slowed down to her natural pace and made sure to keep challenging her without allowing her to become frustrated. It took her until the beginning of third grade before she even began to be what could be considered a fluent reader. She's on the lower side of what is considered normal for her grade level now, but she's making progress, and as long as she is improving I don't worry about it. If she were in a traditional school, she'd be pushed along at the pace of the rest of the classroom instead of being allowed to learn in a way that works for her. The girl who would have been run over and passed by in school is learning and thriving because we kept her at home.

There was a time when we were just beginning when I would have felt a need to label either of these girls in an effort to understand them. I got over that, and I'll bet that you will too. Look for progress, and work towards mastery. There are state standards you can find on your State Board of Education's website. Use these as a measuring stick to see what kinds of things a child should be learning every year. Then realize that every kid is different, and that yours probably won't fall perfectly within the lines. That's completely normal. Know what skills he needs and keep working towards them, but don't beat yourself or your child up if it takes a little longer to get there, or if you feel as if you're running a race to try and keep up.

How do you know the difference between learning disability and disinterest or laziness?

This is really a hard one. Learning disabilities can look like a kid who tries his hardest to do his work and just isn't able to get it done, but it can also look a lot like laziness or boredom. You're going to know which it is the same way the schools would figure it out. You're going to try everything you know to try, and a few things you pull out of thin air, and he's still not going to be able to get it. You are both going to get frustrated. You're going to want to cry and maybe even quit. That's okay – it's a totally normal place to be when you can't help your child. It's a new kind of frustration and a different feeling of helplessness than you've ever known.

So you stop and breathe.

You're not failing him. When the frustration level and the tears tell you that something is wrong, go in search of help. Begin by getting a full medical work-up including vision, allergy, and hearing tests. A large number of "problem students" are children whose issues can be sorted out by an eye doctor, allergist, or pediatrician. A friend of mine is fond of saying "if you hear hoof beats, think horses, not zebras." She's right. Start with the easy stuff before you go looking for more complex problems. By the same token, don't let yourself be easily talked out of looking for more answers. Even hypochondriac moms like me know when there is something wrong with our babies.

If the doctor says everything looks fine and the vision is good or corrected and the issues are still there? Get more information. I don't think you can ever know too much. Your local school district can do the testing for you. They do testing (in most parts of the country) for the private schools in the area, so they can certainly do it for you. The important thing to remember about the schools is that while they are legally required to help you, what they are required to test for are issues that would cause problems in a classroom setting. This is a good beginning, but you may need more information. Your best bet is to find a psychologist, developmental pediatrician, or occupational therapist not affiliated with the school district who specializes in learning disabilities. While it will cost you out of pocket (though it may be covered by insurance, depending on your policy), it is definitely worth the investment in your child's well-being.

Are there homeschool resources that address giving kids coping skills to deal with their learning disabilities?

Yes, it's called her family. Your children are going to take their cues about how they deal with their learning issues from the way that *you* deal with them. Do you use it as an excuse for why your son can't read his history? Does he hear you say that it's because it's too hard? It might *be* too hard, but do you tell him that it is or do you teach him that while it's harder for him, it's a skill he's got to learn? Do you model problem solving skills by looking for solutions and answers and never surrendering?

If your child were diagnosed with a terrible illness, you would research like a mad woman. You would read every book, Google every possibility, and scour the internet for every scrap of information to educate yourself about her condition. Learning disabilities should be treated the same way. Read everything you can lay your hands on, and then go looking for more. You need to become the expert you'd want for your child to have. Some of the information will be insane wackiness, and you'll figure that out very quickly. Sift through the information, and use the experts who are available to you. An occupational therapist can be an invaluable sounding board and source of information. You should use her for that!

You adapt to meet your child's needs. He will require different types of help as he grows, and you have to be able to pivot and meet him where he is. My son with ADHD sits on a yoga ball during school time, because a body in constant motion needs a chair that will move with him. A friend's son wears noise-canceling earphones to deal with his auditory processing disorder. A girl we know uses clear blue plastic overlays to combat double vision and eye-strain. Children with dyslexia can take their tests orally and listen to books on tape, while the child who needs physical stimulation can pace as she reads. By teaching our children to deal effectively with their issues as they do math around the kitchen table, we teach them to pay attention to their own selves, and give them the tools they will need to be successful in life. We learn to modify things for them, so that someday they will learn how to adapt the world to themselves.

How will I know if I'm getting it right?

A child with cognitive issues, whether they are learning issues or sensory issues or whatever, will need for her mom to be her advocate. It wouldn't matter if she were in school or not, she would need for you to be educated, willing to speak up for his best interests, and ready to do whatever it takes to help her succeed. Just keep in mind that her definition of success may not look like success for anyone else.

Success for children with different needs, whether gifted or learning disabled, can be summed up by asking "Is she doing the very best work she's capable of doing?" and "Can she function in the real world?" Can your challenged student balance a checkbook? Is she capable of holding down a job? Can your gifted student hold conversations with real people and not just the running dialogue with Aristotle in her head? The goal of education, for any type of student, is to give her the tools she needs to live a fully engaged and well-informed life. She has to function in the real world when mom isn't there to straighten things out or explain things away.

If you weren't there, how would your child's life look? Have you prepared her and given her the tools to live the life you want her to be able to have? That's the benchmark. Are you doing everything you can to engage her mind and get her excited about learning? At the bottom of it all, it's about teaching the child how to learn. If you do this right, the learning will go on for her entire life, long after you've stopped teaching the lessons.

FOURTEEN

Keeping up with the Housework

If your house is really a mess and a stranger comes to the door, greet him with, "Who could have done this? We have no enemies." – Phyllis Diller

How will I find time for the housework if I'm spending the whole day teaching? I'm a bit afraid of what my house will look like after a whole day at home with me too busy to clean.

Cutting, pasting, and painting can make the efforts of even the best housekeepers look slapdashy, so you're right to be a little afraid of how your house will look when you've spent the day *not* cleaning it. The truth is that it is difficult to have a perfectly spotless house when no one ever leaves it. There have been periods of time where I cringe as I look around after we're done with our schoolwork. While most of the time I can pull it together by bedtime, there have been moments where burning the house to the ground and starting over sounded like a great idea. Even the most meticulous housekeeper is going to find that the way her house looks has changed once she's begun to homeschool. There will be science experiments doing their thing on the counter, and dioramas being built in the dining room. You will have on-going history projects that take over the basement for weeks at a time. These things are all part of educating at home. Teaching people, especially young children, is a messy business. While much of the mess can be cleared up at the end of a long day, there are parts of it that just can't go away at 3:00.

In order to keep your sanity, something's gotta give. That thing should be "being so hard on yourself." Yes, there will be times when you will be the master of complete chaos. There will also be times when everyone is working quietly and you are pleasantly surprised by the way your house looks when you're finished for the day. If you like things to be a certain way, take a moment to look around. Things are going to change once you begin having lessons in your living room. It's going to be different, but that's not always a bad thing.

I'm a bit of a neat freak. I'm not sure how that's going to work.

People change. That doesn't mean that you will be able to ignore the jelly on the kitchen counters, but that you will be able to be more relaxed about how things look in general. It will help if you realize that as a homeschooling family, you are going to be living in your house in a completely different way. You are actually going to *live there* instead of just coming home to it. That makes the way you treat your house a little different. Your house will not only be your quiet refuge at the end of a long day, it will be your place of love, laughter, and learning *throughout* the day. This means that your needs will be completely different from a family whose children leave for school in the morning, while both parents head off to work. Homeschoolers live in our houses in completely different ways than other families, so it makes sense that our houses would look different too.

Now for some nitty-gritty practical tips:

- I have had to remind myself, often, that the mess is harder on my husband than it is on me. (When I say mess, I mean cluttered counters and toys on the floor. If you have slime growing on top of things on your counters...you should do something about that. That's not cool.) He was raised in a pristine household, whereas I was not. I can deal with piles of laundry, and he dreams of floors that are vacuumed daily. That's not going to happen here. I wish it would, but it isn't. He's had to let go of his standard of perfection, and I've had to step up my game. The most important part was our being honest with each other. I had to tell him the reality of my life. Once he got that, it was easier.

- Ask him for his "one thing." What one thing could you make sure was done every day that would serve as the bare minimum? I have friends for whom that minimum is having the bed made daily. Others just want the entry way clean. My own husband asks only that the breakfast bar be wiped off. That's his "good enough." He doesn't complain, and I wipe off the counter just before he gets here.

- Everybody has to help. Even the littlest children should be playing their part in keeping the house as tidy as possible. Teach your children to fold laundry, wash dishes, and mop the floors. It's not selfish to require cooperation. Your goal is to help ease your own burdens so that you have the time to teach them, and to teach them valuable life skills so that someday they will know how to care for themselves.

- Set up a big cleaning rotation so that you're not trying to do everything at once. For example – Mondays wash bed clothes. Tuesdays deep clean the floors. Wednesdays clean the bathrooms. (In our house, the boys clean their own every day. They're boys. Their bathroom needs a daily scrubbing and I don't want to do it.) Clean out the refrigerator every Thursday. Fridays are for grocery shopping. It is well worth the effort to have all of the heavy lifting done so that your weekends are spent having fun. Everyone should get time off, even homeschooling moms. Make sure you schedule some for your family. What a shame it would be to have brilliant children who grew up in a clean house but have no memory of playing with their mom and dad.

- Remember that Mary Poppins was right: a spoonful of sugar really does help the medicine go down. In the case of housework, letting the children choose music-to-clean-by will have your helpers giggling their way through the scrubbing. Turn it into a cleaning dance party. Let out your inner diva and sing a little, Mama! Everything is better when Mom's having fun, and life should be fun, even when mopping the floors.

- Gather the whole family and attack big messes together (while singing to the music of your choice.) If you have four people in your family and you clean for 15 minutes, that's an hour of cleaning on that one room. That's guaranteed to make a dent in even the biggest mess.

- Set a time limit. I am a firm believer in the adage that you can do anything, no matter how distasteful, if you know when it's going to end (and *that* it's going to end!). Your children are the same way, only with shorter attention spans and without your sense of purpose when it comes to cleaning. Round them all up. Start with one room, set an egg timer, and you'll see mountains moving at your house... mountains of clutter.

What about laundry?

Ah, laundry, that never-ending chore. With nine people living in our house, the laundry is never going to be finished. I've tried hard to make peace with that fact. It helped the day that I realized laundry was a skill the children need to learn. It's one more homeschooling lesson in Home Ec 101. They need to be able to wash their own clothes. I can't even tell you how many of my fellow college freshmen a thousand years ago stood in front of washing machines reading the detergent labels, trying to figure out how it all worked. Don't let your child be that guy! If he's tall enough to reach the bottom of the washing machine, he's old enough to wash his own clothes.

It helps to assign laundry days for each of the older children, during which you expect them to wash and dry their clothes and bed sheets, fold them, and put them away. You should be nearby to lend a hand, to help with ironing, or to give advice, but this is theirs to do. You'll notice that they take more pride in how they look, and are better about putting their clothes away carefully when it becomes their own responsibility.

I still do the linens and clothing for the littler kids, unless my husband beats me to it. That's part of the secret of our success around here. My husband does laundry, and does it well. We spend most of our TV watching time in the evenings folding whatever laundry was washed that day. The goal is always to have all the laundry finished by the time he gets home on Friday. That way, we get the weekend off. We don't always make it, but I hope for it every week. (If you don't live in a household with nine people, this should be an easily attainable goal. If we can make it most weeks, then I know you can too.)

So the house is clean-ish and the laundry is done. I still have to feed them. Where do I find the time to cook?

Feeding a family three meals a day, plus snacks, seven days a week is a daunting task. It's the one place where moms whose children are in school get it easy. Their children are eating at least one meal at school. Feeding the children never seems to stop. No sooner will you have cleared away the dishes from lunch before you'll have to think about what to defrost for dinner. I hate feeling overwhelmed by food preparation because I dearly love to cook, and I'm darn good at it. Unfortunately, I don't always have the time to do it the way I would like to, and that can be discouraging.

I was beginning to give up hope and just resign myself to the fact that the pizza guy knows all my children by name when I discovered the wonder of a slow cooker. (It's a crock pot if you're in Texas.) It wasn't that I didn't own one or that I had never used it before then – I used it for pot roast. It was just that I had no idea how versatile it could be. The afternoon I discovered that I could make chicken nuggets and smoked ribs in the crock pot changed my life forever.

There are whole websites devoted to crock pot cooking and thousands of recipes you can try on your family. Some of my favorite sites to try are:

- *http://crockpot365.blogspot.com/*

- *http://www.crock-pot.com/Recipes.aspx*

- *http://www.momswhothink.com/crock-pot-recipes/crock-pot-recipes-for-the-crockpot-and-slow-cooker.html*

- *http://southernfood.about.com/library/crock/blcpidx.htm*

What I love about the slow cooker is that all the hard work can be done ahead of time. After you put the children in bed or in the morning before school begins, get the prep work out of the way. If you put the food in after breakfast, you won't have to think about it again until it's time to eat. It isn't effortless cooking, but it's darn close. If you spend the extra money for disposable crock pot liner bags, then there isn't even a mess to clean up. How great is dinner without a mess?

The crock pot? That's your big idea?

Don't knock it 'til you try it, sister. It's all kinds of wonderful, but it won't make your life any easier unless you plan your meals ahead of time. That crock pot might be kitchen magic, but if you don't know what you're making until 30 minutes before meal time, then it's just a fancy dust catcher. I don't know about you, but I have enough of those already. That means you have to take a half hour or so every week or two (depending on how often you shop) for menu planning. It's not the most fun thing you're going to do this week, but it's one of the most important.

Open up your freezer and take stock of what you have on hand. Next, check the calendar and see what you have planned for each day, that way you can match fast-and-easy to the busiest day and keep the slower stuff for when you have more time. Make a list of what you're going to eat and what you need to pick up the next time you're at the store. A planned outing to the zoo means that you need easy snack stuff you can pack like grapes and baby carrots (and those little bags of chips and fruit snacks!) The nights you have practices or classes until late will call for something that will be done early enough to be eaten before they go and light enough to not make them sick. (Quesadillas or grilled cheese sandwiches. Hooray!) Those rare nights when you have no plans at all, have something you all love so you enjoy just being with your family. Having three meals a day planned in advance can help keep you calm and sane. Posting it where your children can read it will (maybe) stop their constant questions about what's for dinner.

In addition to all the meal planning, make some room in your budget for snacks. Little bodies in motion need lots of fuel. Make sure to have an ample supply of whatever kinds of snacks are acceptable in your house. You'll be surprised at the kind of appetite learning can work up in a kid.

Anything else?

You bet! I also think that feeding the family is another area for teaching life skills. By 10 or 11, most children can make very basic foods like spaghetti with meat sauce or chicken tacos. This can be a life saver for you. On those days when the baby is sick and refuses to be put down, you can sit on the rocker and hold her for most of the day and know that someone else is capable of making dinner. The last time it happened to me, I was very fortunate to have a 12-year-old who knows how to brown hamburger meat, chop veggies, shred a bit of cheese, and ended up making some pretty tasty loaded nachos for dinner. I supervised as best as I could from the next room, but the crafting of dinner was all his as was the praise of his little brothers and sister when he served it to them. He beamed with pleasure at their praise and thanked me for letting him cook! Here he was helping me out, and he thought it was a privilege! If we are forever doing things for our children and not teaching them to do for themselves, then we are doing them a disservice. Not only are we not teaching them what they need to know in life, we are robbing them of the opportunity to excel.

FIFTEEN

Maintaining Your Identity

Today you are You, that is truer than true. There is no one alive who is Youer than You." – Dr. Seuss

When I think about homeschooling moms, a stereotype immediately pops into my head. I'm a little afraid of becoming that girl. Is it possible to do this and still be me? I really don't want to end up as some sort of bad cliché.

I think I know the stereotype you mean. Does is contain the words "denim jumper?" It's funny to me that such a diverse group of people has somehow become defined by one article of clothing. Most stereotypes contain some truth, and this one does as well.

In the beginning, most of the homeschooling moms were fundamentalist Christian moms (well, actually, the first homeschoolers were probably the hippies – then the Christians took over and made it HUGE). Folks of the fundamentalist persuasion tend to follow certain rules regarding how they dress. Those rules included dresses and skirts for women. When you're chasing small children all day long, denim just seems to make sense from a practical standpoint, and – Voila! – we have denim jumpers on the moms. The image of those early homeschooling pioneers got stuck in our collective imaginations and now the term "homeschooler" immediately brings to mind "denim jumpers." Those women are still out here, making up a noticeable swath of the homeschool community. The vast majority of them are some of the kindest and most humble women you will ever have the privilege to meet.

That doesn't mean that you have to wear a jumper in order to teach your children. The homeschool movement has become so large that it now includes every kind of mom. I've swapped literature suggestions with moms with facial piercing and wild tattoos, and discussed grammar with Mennonites in their long skirts and caps. We run the gamut from looking like a regular mom to any kind of wild extreme you can imagine. So, don't even worry about it. Whatever your particular brand of odd happens to be, you'll find your niche and be just fine.

Do you feel pressure from other moms to conform?

Absolutely. Not just from homeschool moms, but from women in general. I've learned in all my interactions with other women that women are like zebras. It's not that we like stripes; it's that we have a natural instinct to try and blend in. There is safety in that big mass of "everyone looks the same", and we like it. It's the only excuse I can come up with for the mile high hair of the late 80s and early 90s. We knew we looked ridiculous, but we did it anyway. The girls who didn't were treated mercilessly by the rest of the herd.

There was one summer where I thought purple streaks in my hair sounded like a fun thing to try. I rocked those purple highlights! At the first homeschool group meeting after I had them done, I heard a collective gasp as I walked into the room. The next morning I got an email removing me from the board because I had "developed questionable personal judgment." After nine years of teaching at home, I was removed from the board of a group I had founded because I rocked the boat. I knew what was going on. They were playing the girl version of Whack-a-Mole, where anyone who sticks out from the crowd gets thumped. I sat at the computer that morning and laughed at the ridiculousness of it. I liked my hair. My husband liked it. I didn't much care what the "old guard" thought.

I'm not sure what it is about women that makes us uncomfortable around the unusual and unique. I am not sure why we don't trust people who are true to themselves. It doesn't seem to matter very much where you are, or what line of work you're in, looking like everyone else carries with it some social safety. If you need that, I'm pretty sure someone will be happy to tell you where to buy your jumper. If you don't need that and you'd rather wear your zebra stripes with glitter, or if your brain just works better when you're wearing a tiara, don't apologize for it! Put that tiara on your head, girl, and go teach something!

If you want my opinion (and you bought my book so I might as well tell you), becoming a homeschooling cliché is the wrong thing to fret over. I think you should worry about becoming beige.

Beige?

Moms who have children (That's all of us!) have a tendency to put the care of the rest of the world ahead of the care of ourselves. Over time, that neglect takes hold and the moms just start to fade. Their natural brilliance disappears and they become the color of the wall. These once vibrant women start to blend into the background of their own lives, lost and forgotten...invisible. What begins out of love and selflessness ends up turning mom beige. It doesn't end up as a kind or loving thing at all. It ends up as self-neglect, and that's not a great example to set for the kids.

We owe it to ourselves and to our families to hold tightly to the women that we are. Our husbands fell in love with the girl who stood next to him at the altar. Our children are their own wonderful quirky selves precisely because of who we are. I'd hate for them to lose that. So don't become beige –and you know what I mean – frazzled hair and cookie-slimed sweaters. If your "good shirt" is just the one that's clean, it's time to take better care of yourself.

There's the other kind of beige too, the kind where you can't discuss anything other than childbirth and baby poop. Can you talk about other things? Do you know what's going on in the world outside your front door? I once sat next to my husband's coworker at a dinner party. He asked me what was going on in my life, and I answered something about a friend of mine being pregnant with her eighth baby. I didn't know what else to say. He rudely sneered and said "Why would I care about that?" and didn't talk to me again for the rest of the evening. It was hurtful and humiliating, *and* one of the most valuable lessons I've ever learned. You have to be able to talk to real people in the real world, so you need to have a clue about what kinds of things interest non-homeschooling people.

How do you find time for taking care of yourself? Do you rely on your spouse? Babysitters? Family? All of the above? I'm swamped already.

You have to make it a priority. Your idea of self-care can be anything from getting your eyebrows threaded (for me $7 is money well spent to take my Sasquatch brows down to something prettier), meeting up at the local coffee shop for an hour of good conversation with a friend, or slipping out to the library for some quiet reading time. We're all happier people when we give ourselves at least a bare minimum of care. That contentment will spill over into every part of your life. The hassle of carving out that time alone is an investment with great returns.

If Step 1 is deciding to do it, then Step 2 is making a plan. I actually have to write what I'm doing on the calendar or it's never going to happen. We have a saying in our house that if it's not on the calendar, it doesn't exist. But once it's up there in ink, my family just considers it a given that I'm going to do whatever it says.

Your next obstacle will be childcare. At this point in my life, I'm blessed to have two children who are old enough to babysit. That simplifies things quite a bit, and I definitely take advantage of it. If you're not there yet, there are all kinds of strategies for finding time for yourself. For me, my husband was absolutely the go-to guy. When the kids were little I would make it a point to get up to run at 6 a.m. because he was still home, and schedule hair appointments on Saturdays because I could slip out and leave Dad in charge. If that's not feasible for whatever reason (he works wonky hours, he travels a lot, etc.), and you don't have family nearby who are willing to lend you a hand (I understand grandmas are great for this!), you might try arranging a baby swap with a close friend or neighbor. She could take yours on Tuesday afternoons, and you'll watch hers on Thursdays... whatever works with your schedule.

Even the days when you don't leave the house, try to carve out a little bit of "me" time. Shush the big kids and send them out to play during naptimes so you can dance like a fool to 80s music, read Shakespeare or watch some TV. If it's your thing, slip away after the children are in bed and take a long, hot bath. Don't underestimate the value of hot water, bubbles, music, and a locked door to lift your spirit. I have certainly had days in which the hot bath at the end *was* my sanity.

Do you ever feel selfish or like you're taking something away from your family when you spend the time and money on yourself?

No. I used to, but...now? No. It's the silliest thing really, this notion that moms who do nice things for themselves are somehow selfish or bad.

I have a sweet friend who rented a cello for herself last year. She has always wanted to learn to play, but didn't think she could afford one. She was surprised to learn that the monthly rental was about the same as the price of taking her family out to eat one fast food meal. She vowed to cook more, brought home her cello, and began to teach herself to play. She was happier with herself than she could remember being. Her children bragged on their mom. Her husband followed her lead and rented a violin. He began to teach himself to play. After a while, they played screeching duets in the evening after the children went to bed. This little splurge on herself brought such joy to her household. It was some of the best time and money she ever spent.

If it makes you happy and your family is not suffering – and giving up a meal of fast-food burgers is not suffering – then go for it! Do the little things that make you happy, and give those big dreams a try. It will only serve to enrich your family's life, and there's nothing selfish at all about that.

Anything else?

Never underestimate the value of a set bedtime for your kids. I don't care what age your kids are – the older ones can have extra reading time in their rooms if 9:30 seems too early for them to turn in. This is your job and you need to be able to clock out at the end of the day. Like any job, there will be late night emergencies and unplanned events, but around here we're a bit fanatical about bedtimes.

Putting the children in bed at 8:30 for the littles and 9:00 for the bigs means that every evening I get an hour or more to curl up on the couch with my beloved. Sometimes we talk, more often we read or watch TV, but that's not the point. We get to be "just us" for a little while. He's still the cute boy I fell in love with, and I like to hang out with him. Having a set kid-bedtime lets that happen.

I know there are lots of families who let their children stay up late, and I would ask you to please re-think that strategy unless you have a concrete reason for doing so (like dad doesn't get home until 9:00 and the kids hang out with him for a while.) The children will be better prepared for the school day if they've had a full night's sleep and you will be a happier woman if you actually get an end to your day. Give it a try. You might like it.

Have you found other homeschooling moms who are struggling to hold onto themselves too? Do you talk about it?

Yes, we talk about it. Often. It's painful to realize that you have gotten lost in the Land of Beige. I've never met a mom of any kind who wasn't struggling at least a bit to maintain her identity. The change from girl or woman to Mother is a huge leap and there's no warning or preparation for it. With this redefinition of self and societal pressure to define "Mom" a certain way, it's easy to forget all the plans and dreams we have for ourselves. It's daunting to set out to re-discover who you are now on your own and not just in relation to the short people living in your house. It will take some time and a bit of an effort, but it's a journey of discovery that it is absolutely essential for you to make.

We, as moms, need to help each other hang on to those dreams and to dream even bigger for ourselves. This isn't selfishness! This is setting a good example for our children. Would you be happy to see your daughter get married, have babies, and then fade into beige until she blended in with the walls? Heck no! You would smack her upside the head and ask her "What on earth are you doing?" Take a good look in the mirror. That girl is someone's beloved daughter. She deserves better than beige.

Final Thoughts

If you've read this whole book from one end to the other, or in any random order you chose, you have a pretty good soup-to-nuts idea of what it really looks like to teach your children at home. I hope you've also come to realize that mothers who successfully educate their own children aren't some kind of perfect character out of a story book. We aren't paragons of anything. We're just moms who love our children and want what is in their best interest. In our families, "best interest" means that we're teaching them in the dining room.

There is no one specific stereotype that fits all homeschooling mothers. Throw out your thoughts of denim jumpers and realize that we're every kind of mom. We are the uber-organized and the super slacker, the deep thinker and the mom with ADD, the highly motivated mom, and the one who's lazy as snail snot. Don't think that because you are who you are you can't do what we do. You can.

Here are a few final thoughts as you get started:

- Pray, pray, pray. And when you're done, another quick one wouldn't hurt you.

- Be kind to yourself. You don't have to be the perfect teacher for your children to learn.

- Be honest with yourself about who you are. You can't even start to think about what works for your children until you know what works for you.

- Be willing to change your opinion about what works for you.

- Recognize that the way your family lives inside your house is going to change. Decide right now to be okay with that.

- Don't get overwhelmed. You're not making a commitment to do anything for the next however many years. Make a commitment for this year, or even just this semester, and see how it goes.

- Re-evaluate regularly in your first years. You can change the curricula. You can change your schedule. You can change your methods and approach, so be honest about what's going on. Don't keep flogging a dead horse.

- Please know that there is no shame in admitting that the horse really is dead and climbing off.

- Give yourself and your child a chance for it to work. Don't give up after one week, or after four or five when the honeymoon period is over. Be patient with yourself and your student(s). This is new for everyone involved and there will be a learning curve.

- Don't belittle yourself for "not being patient enough" to homeschool. Patience is a muscle; the more you use it the stronger it gets.

- Don't belittle yourself for "not being smart enough" to homeschool. Some of the most brilliant women I know never went to college; a diploma doesn't prove intelligence. Can you read? You're smart enough. Remember that you will own the teacher manuals, so you don't need to know it all. (Breathe a big sigh of relief here.)

- No matter how great a school is, no teacher is ever going to care as much about the success of your children as much as you do. There are great, heroic teachers out there. They are not as passionate about your children as you are. This is definitely in your favor.

- Remember that all children are created equal but different. Completely different. There is no cookie cutter approach to a child's brain.

- Never, never, never judge one child's progress by the accomplishment of another child, especially if that other child is not in your home. One of the things I've learned about other kids' progress is that, sometimes, moms don't tell you the whole truth.

- Set realistic goals for yourself. What is your purpose? Do you want to turn out mini-geniuses who go on Letterman or do you want to raise kind, faithful, caring human beings who have the skills necessary to succeed in life? Teach toward the end result you want.

- Remind yourself that no one needs to know everything by the time they're five years old.

- Remember that as important as this new job of homeschooling is, it's not your only one. You still need to be a good wife, a good friend, a loving mom, a semi-decent house-keeper, and you. Don't resign from those other things just because you decided to be a home educator.

- Did I mention that you need to pray? Yeah...that's never a bad idea. In fact, you might want to do that again.

Whether you've been homeschooling for a couple years now or you're just beginning today, you already *are* the teacher. It's not the curriculum, experience, or the paperwork you've filled out that makes it so. You're your kids' mom – that's what makes you their teacher. The fact is, you've been teaching your children from the very beginning of their lives. You've got this. You already know more about teaching than you think you do. You're not doing something revolutionary here; you're just adding academics to the long list of things that your children are already learning from you.

It doesn't matter if you're the kind of mom who wears a tiara to teach World History or a denim jumper, the key to successful homeschooling is to enjoy your children and to be true to the woman that you are. Remember to keep your eyes on God, to be honest about where you are, and to dance every step of the way to whatever weird and wonderful tune gets your feet in motion.

A Few Helpful Links to Get You Started

Book Suppliers

Catholic

All Catholic Books* – acbooks.net

Aquinas Homeschool Books – catholichomeschool.com

Arma Dei – armadei.com

Bethlehem Books – bethelehembooks.com

Blue Mantle Educational Supplies (Canada) – bluemantle.ca

Emmanuel Books – emmanuelbooks.com

My Catholic Faith Delivered – mycatholicfaithdelivered.com

Neumann Press – neumannpress.com

RACE for Heaven (Catholic Living Books) – raceforheaven.com

Sacred Heart Books and Gifts* - sacredheartbooksandgifts.com

Saint Francis Books (Canada) – stfrancisbooks.com

*Offers discount to homeschoolers

Other Christian

A Brighter Child – abrighterchild.com

AbeBooks – abebooks.com

Christian Book – christianbook.com/homeschool

Christian Homeschool Books – homeschool-books.com

Grace and Truth - graceandtruthbooks.com/category/homeschool-resources

Homeschool Supercenter – homeschoolsupercenter.com

Homeschooling Books – homeschoolingbooks.com

Mardel Book Stores – mardel.com/Homeschool.aspx

Rainbow Resource – rainbowresource.com

Secular

A Brighter Child – abrighterchild.com

Amazon – amazon.com

Barnes & Noble* – barnesandnoble.com

BiblioMania – bibliomaniatulsa.com

Rainbow Resource – rainbowresource.com

The BackPack (used text books) – thebackpack.com/

Usborne – usbornehoemschoolbooks.com

Used Homeschooling Books – usedhomeschoolbooks.com

Curriculum

Catholic

Angelicum Academy –angelicum.net

By Way of the Family – bywayofthefamily.com

Catholic Heritage Curriculum –catholichomeschooling.com

Catholic Icing (Preschool) – catholicicing.com

Homeschool Connections – homeschoolconnectionsonline.com

Koble Academy Home School –kolbe.org

Little Saints Catholic Preschool Program – catholicpreschool.com

Our Lady of the Rosary School – olrs.com/index.html

Our Lady of Victory Catholic Homeschool Curriculum – olvs.org

Saint Thomas Aquinas Academy – staa-homeschool.com

Seton Home Study School – setonhome.org

The Rolling Acres School – therollingacresfarm.com/school

Other Christian

Abeka – abeka.com/HomeSchool/Default.aspx

Alpha Omega – aopschools.com

Calvert School – homeschool.calvertschool.org

Clonlara School Home Based Education Program – clonlara.org

Cornerstone Curriculum – cornerstonecurriculum.com

Geo Matters – homes-school-curriculum.com

Love to Learn – lovetolearn.net

My Father's World – mfwbooks.com

Oak Meadow School – oakmeadow.com

Sonlight – sonlight.com

Tapestry of Grace – tapestryofgrace.com

Timberdoodle Co – timberdoodle.com

Secular

K12 – k12.com

Enki Education – enkieducation.org

Usborne – usbornehoemschoolbooks.com

Educational Materials

Enchanted Learning – enchantedlearning.com

Joan's Company – teachmestuff.com

Lord of History – lordofhistory.com

Traditional Catholic Art and Homeschool Materials – traditionalcatholicart.com

Fun Stuff

Barinya (photography) – barinya.com/educational/activities/photography/index.ht m

Catholic Icing – catholicicing.com

Illuminated Ink – illuminatedink.com

That Artist Woman – thatartistwoman.com

The Warrenton Quarterly – warrentonquarterly.webs.com

Lapbooking

Hands of a Child – handsofachild.com

Homeschool Share – homeschoolshare.com

Lapbooks for Catholics – lapbooksforcatholics.com

Message Boards

Catholic

4Real (Catholic Charlotte Mason group) – 4real.thenetsmith.com

Ora et Labora (private) – oroetlaboro.yuku.com/login/loginnow/Login-to-Yuku.html

Other Christian

Christian Homeschool Fellowship – chfweb.com

Homeschool Christian – homeschoolchristian.com/forum/category-view.asp

Homeschool.com – homeschool.com/forum/

Teaching Mom– teachingmom.com/boards/

The Homeschool Lounge – thehomeschoollounge.com

Secular

About.com –
forums.about.com/n/pfx/forum.aspx?nav=messages&webtag=ab-homeschool

iVillage – ivillage.com/forums/forum/20149

Music

Alan Jensen Music – aljem.com

Making Music Praying Twice –
makingmusicprayingtwice.com

Resources

Catholic

El Camino Real (The Royal Road) – lcaminoreal.org

Homeschool Faith and Family Life –
thebestofhomeschoolfaithandfamilylife.com

Love 2 Learn – love2learn.net

That Resource Site – thatresourcesite.com

Other

1+1+1=1 – 1plus1plus1equals1.com

Children's Encyclopedia –
academickids.com/encyclopedia/index.php/Main_Page

Confessions of a Homeschooler –
confessionsofahomeschooler.com

Donna Young Printables and Resources –
donnayoung.org/index.htm

Homeschool Creations – homeschoolcreations.net

Mercy Academy Learning Styles Test -
67.252.113.51/mercyacademy/

Standardized Testing

Brewer Testing Services – brewertesting.com

CHAP Online – chaponline.com/choosing-and-ordering-standardized-tests

Kid TEST – kidtest.com

Time 4 Learning (test prep) – time4learning.com/testprep/

Tutoring , Academic Mentoring, and Study Guides

Aleks – aleks.com

Aquinas Learning – aquinaslearning.com

Caedmon Tutorials – caedmontutorials.com

Hillside Education – hillsideeducation.com/index.html

Kahn Academy – khanacademy.org

Writing-Edu – excellenceinwriting.com

Acknowledgements

Books don't happen in a vacuum y'all. There are a few people who had a hand in this that I need to thank:

First of all, I am grateful to Our Heavenly Father for the gifts of family, friends, knowledge, and a need to write which have made this book possible.

Thank you to my understanding husband who dragged seven reluctant children out of the house in all kinds of weather so that I could have a quiet house in which to write. To Madelyne, Wyatt, Lincoln, Ella, Cullen, Bob, and Josephine who have weathered the storm of having an author for a mom. Your understanding that my using the computer for writing is more important than video games has helped this book to take four months longer to write than I had planned. I love you all madly. You are the reason I sing in the kitchen and dance up the stairs.

Beth Pack – my own personal Jiminy Cricket – my writing conscience, thank you for keeping me on track. To Kim Davis – thank you for your "appalling lack of curiosity" which helped to provide the skeleton on which this book is built, and for being my BFF before BFF was a thing. We were the best unicorns ever! Thank you to Abigail Benjamin – the most enthusiastic cheerleader a girl could hope to have. And, Alexis Walkenstein who prayed me through the rough bits and gave me the gumption to get to work! A big shout out to Ellen Hrkach, my book coach, who walked me through this a step at a time.

To my four dear friends who never tired of hearing about this project (or never told me if they did) – Scottie Vosburgh who is unflinchingly honest and let me drive her car even after I got a speeding ticket in it. Kara Allen who helps me to fill in the blanks and is the adult voice I call when I'm under the bed and hiding from the children. Carrie Golladay who has supported my need to write from the very beginning and appreciates my love of peeenk (with the three e's) even when she doesn't understand it. Carolyn Parham who snaps me out of a brain-drain stupor with a mug of salted caramel hot chocolate as she regales me with the harrowing tales of her past. – Thank you. My life is lived in Technicolor because of the four of you.

Thank you to my brilliant and patient editor Suzan Sammons, who might smack me if I ever write "which" or "a bit" again. Without you this book would only be a shadow of what it is today. Thank you for pushing me to "be the expert" and to get the ADD out of my writing.

Thank you to the brave volunteers who read the abysmal rough draft and gave me candid and thought-provoking feedback:

Larry Deninger, Katie Engebretsen, Karey Nobles, Leah Gaines, Erin Lane, Brook Alcorn, Sarah Reinhard, and Christina Yeary.

Thank you to Mike Doyle who looked for typos. If there are any in the book, it's his fault. A huge thank you to Joy Tolley who took the cover photo and to Jon Benjamin who made it look like the cover of a book.